The Wiersbe
BIBLE STUDY SERIES

The
Wiersbe
BIBLE STUDY SERIES

2 SAMUEL & I CHRONICLES

Trusting God

to See Us

Through

David C Cook®

transforming lives together

THE WIERSBE BIBLE STUDY SERIES: 2 SAMUEL AND 1 CHRONICLES
Published by David C Cook
4050 Lee Vance View
Colorado Springs, CO 80918 U.S.A.

David C Cook Distribution Canada
55 Woodslee Avenue, Paris, Ontario, Canada N3L 3E5

David C Cook U.K., Kingsway Communications
Eastbourne, East Sussex BN23 6NT, England

The graphic circle C logo is a registered trademark of David C Cook.

All excerpts taken from *Be Restored*, second edition, published by David C
Cook in 2010 © 2002 Warren W. Wiersbe, ISBN 978-1-4347-0049-0.

ISBN 978-0-7814-1039-7
eISBN 978-0-7814-1279-7

The Team: Karen Lee-Thorp, Amy Konyndyk, Nick Lee, Jack Campbell, Karen Athen
Series Cover Design: John Hamilton Design
Cover Photo: iStockphoto

Printed in the United States of America
First Edition 2015

1 2 3 4 5 6 7 8 9 10

112714

Contents

Introduction to 2 Samuel and 1 Chronicles

David's Story

Second Samuel begins with the death of Saul, Israel's first king, and ends with the death of David, Israel's greatest king. The book tells how God enabled David to unite the twelve tribes into one nation, defeat their enemies, expand their borders, and prepare the way for Solomon to ascend the throne. Parallel passages in 1 Chronicles supplement the "prophetic" account in 2 Samuel and give us the priestly point of view.

One of the major themes of 2 Samuel is restoration—the restoration of national unity, the restoration of David after he sinned, and the restoration of the throne after Absalom's rebellion. Intertwined with this theme is the emphasis on power, showing how God empowered David and His people to accomplish His will. Saul tore things apart, but God used David to start putting things back together again.

Restoration

If the life of David teaches us anything, it's that God can use imperfect people to accomplish His purposes, though He lovingly disciplines when His servants disobey Him. David was a "man after [God's] own heart"

(1 Sam. 13:14); but David was still a man, and he knew the weaknesses of human flesh. Second Samuel also teaches us that no personal or national situation is beyond the Lord's ability to put things right. David's legacy was a united people and a strong kingdom. He turned over to his son Solomon all he needed to do the one thing David wanted to do more than anything else—build a temple for the Lord.

We live in a shattered and fragmented world, and God's eternal goal is to bring all things together in Christ (Eph. 1:10). God is looking for men and women who will yield to His power and help restore broken lives, homes, churches, cities, and nations. Are you available?

—*Warren . Wiersbe*

How to Use This Study

This study is designed for both individual and small-group use. We've divided it into eight lessons—each references one or more chapters in Warren W. Wiersbe's commentary *Be Restored* (second edition, David C Cook, 2010). While reading *Be Restored* is not a prerequisite for going through this study, the additional insights and background Wiersbe offers can greatly enhance your study experience.

The **Getting Started** questions at the beginning of each lesson offer you an opportunity to record your first thoughts and reactions to the study text. This is an important step in the study process as those "first impressions" often include clues about what it is your heart is longing to discover.

The bulk of the study is found in the **Going Deeper** questions. These dive into the Bible text and, along with helpful excerpts from Wiersbe's commentary, help you examine not only the original context and meaning of the verses but also modern application.

Looking Inward narrows the focus down to your personal story. These intimate questions can be a bit uncomfortable at times, but don't shy away from honesty here. This is where you are asked to stand before the mirror of God's Word and look closely at what you see. It's the place to take a good look at yourself in light of the lesson and search for ways in which you can grow in faith.

Going Forward is the place where you can commit to paper those things you want or need to do in order to better live out the discoveries you made in the Looking Inward section. Don't skip or skim through this. Take the time to really consider what practical steps you might take to move closer to Christ. Then share your thoughts with a trusted friend who can act as an encourager and accountability partner.

Finally, there is a brief **Seeking Help** section to close the lesson. This is a reminder for you to invite God into your spiritual-growth process. If you choose to write out a prayer in this section, come back to it as you work through the lesson and continue to seek the Holy Spirit's guidance as you discover God's will for your life.

Tips for Small Groups

A small group is a dynamic thing. One week it might seem like a group of close-knit friends. The next it might seem more like a group of uncomfortable strangers. A small-group leader's role is to read these subtle changes and adjust the tone of the discussion accordingly.

Small groups need to be safe places for people to talk openly. It is through shared wrestling with difficult life issues that some of the greatest personal growth is discovered. But in order for the group to feel safe, participants need to know it's okay *not* to share sometimes. Always invite honest disclosure, but never force someone to speak if he or she isn't comfortable doing so. (A savvy leader will follow up later with a group member who isn't comfortable sharing in a group setting to see if a one-on-one discussion is more appropriate.)

Have volunteers take turns reading excerpts from Scripture or from the commentary. The more each person is involved even in the mundane tasks, the more they'll feel comfortable opening up in more meaningful ways.

The leader should watch the clock and keep the discussion moving. Sometimes there may be more Going Deeper questions than your group can cover in your available time. If you've had a fruitful discussion, it's okay to move on without finishing everything. And if you think the group is getting bogged down on a question or has taken off on a tangent, you can simply say, "Let's go on to question 5." Be sure to save at least ten to fifteen minutes for the Going Forward questions.

Finally, soak your group meetings in prayer—before you begin, during as needed, and always at the end of your time together.

King of Judah
(2 SAMUEL 1—4; 1 CHRONICLES 10:1–12)

Before you begin …
- *Pray for the Holy Spirit to reveal truth and wisdom as you go through this lesson.*
- *Read 2 Samuel 1—4 and 1 Chronicles 10:1–12. This lesson references chapters 1 and 2 in* Be Restored. *It will be helpful for you to have your Bible and a copy of the commentary available as you work through this lesson.*

Getting Started

From the Commentary

For ten years David was an exile with a price on his head, fleeing from Saul and waiting for the time when God would put him on the throne of Israel. During those difficult years, David grew in faith and godly character, and God equipped him for the work He had chosen for him to do. When the day of victory did arrive, David was careful not to force himself on the people, many of whom were still loyal to the house of Saul. He took a cautious approach, and we can't help but admire David for his wisdom and patience as he won the affection and allegiance of the people and sought to unify the shattered nation. "So he shepherded them according to the integrity of his heart, and guided them by the skillfulness of his hands" (Ps. 78:72 NKJV).

—*Be Restored*, page 17

1. What was David's "cautious approach" to the people? How did he win their affection and loyalty? (See 2 Sam. 1; 2:4–7; 3:28–39; 4:9–12.) What lessons can we take from his example for how to lead in the church today?

2. Choose one verse or phrase from 2 Samuel 1—4 or 1 Chronicles 10:1–12 that stands out to you. This could be something you're intrigued by, something that makes you uncomfortable, something that puzzles you, something that resonates with you, or just something you want to examine further. Write that here.

Going Deeper

From the Commentary

On the day that David was slaughtering the Amalekites, the Philistines were overpowering Saul and his army at Mount Gilboa, where they killed Saul and three of his sons (1 Sam. 31; 1 Chron. 10). The next day, while David was returning to Ziklag, the Philistines were humiliating Saul by desecrating his body and the bodies of his sons, and the Amalekite messenger was starting off to bring the news to David. It took him at least three days to get to Ziklag, which was about eighty miles from the scene of the battle. So it was on David's third day in Ziklag that he received the tragic news that Israel had been defeated and that Saul and three of his sons were dead.

Scripture gives us three accounts of the death of Saul and his sons: 1 Samuel 31, the report of the messenger in 2 Samuel 1:1–10, and the record in 1 Chronicles 10. According to 1 Chronicles 10:4, Saul killed himself by falling on his sword, but the messenger said he had killed Saul to save him from experiencing further agony and humiliation. First Chronicles 10:14 informs us that it was God who killed Saul for his rebellion, especially the sin of seeking guidance from a medium. Only with great difficulty can the reports in 1 Samuel 31 and 1 Chronicles 10 be reconciled with the report of the messenger; therefore, it's likely the man was lying.

There's no question that the man had been on the battlefield. While he was searching for spoils, he found the corpses of Saul and his sons before the Philistines had identified them, and he took Saul's insignias of kingship: his golden armband and the gold chaplet he wore on his helmet. However, the Amalekite didn't kill Saul as he claimed, because Saul and his sons were already dead. But by claiming that he did, he lost his own life.

One of the key words in 2 Samuel 1 is *fallen*, found in verses 4, 10, 12, 19, 25, and 27. When Saul began his royal career, he was described as standing head and shoulders "taller than any of the people" (1 Sam. 9:2 NASB; see 1 Sam. 10:23 and 16:7), but he ended his career a fallen king. He fell on his face in fear in the house of the spirit medium (1 Sam. 28:20), and he fell on the battlefield before the enemy (1 Sam. 31:4). David humbled himself before the Lord, and the Lord lifted him up; but Saul's pride and rebellion brought him to a shameful end. "Therefore let him who thinks he stands take heed lest he fall" (1 Cor. 10:12 NKJV). Saul was anointed king at the dawning of a new day (1 Sam. 9:26), but he chose to walk in the darkness (1 Sam. 28:8) and disobey the will of God.

—*Be Restored*, pages 18–19

3. Review 2 Samuel 1:1–10. Why would the Amalekite lie about killing Saul? What happened to Saul that turned him into a fallen man? (See 1 Sam. 13:11–14.) How is his story similar to other biblical characters' falls from grace? What are some parallels in Saul's story to the temptations church leaders face today?

More to Consider: In slaying the messenger, David vindicated Saul and his sons and demonstrated publicly that he had not been Saul's enemy and did not rejoice at Saul's death. Why was this a dangerous thing to do? How might David's decision to stand with the dead king of Israel be considered an act of treason? How did the conduct of David and his camp on this issue affect the way his future subjects would perceive him?

From the Commentary

David's grief over the death of Saul and Jonathan was sincere, and to help the people remember them, he wrote a touching elegy in their honor. He ordered this lament to be taught and sung in his ancestral tribe of Judah, and no doubt people in other tribes learned and appreciated it. The people of the East unashamedly display their emotions, and their poets frequently write songs to help them commemorate both joyful and painful experiences. Moses taught Israel a song to warn them about apostasy (Deut. 32), and the prophets often wrote funeral dirges to announce impending judgment (Isa. 14:12ff.; Ezek. 27:1ff.; 28:11–19).

This lament came to be known as "The Song of the Bow" (2 Sam. 1:18) and was recorded in the book of Jasher (Josh. 10:12–13), a collection of poems and songs that commemorated great events in the history of Israel. "How are the mighty fallen" is the major theme of the elegy (2 Sam. 1:19, 25, 27), and the emphasis is on the greatness of Saul and Jonathan even in defeat and death. David celebrated their skill and bravery and their willingness to give their lives for their country. Like Hebrews 11, nothing is recorded in the song that speaks of any sins or mistakes in the lives of Saul and Jonathan.

—*Be Restored*, pages 20–21

4. What was the purpose of public lamentation in Old Testament times? How did David lament Saul and Jonathan—what did he say about them? How does the modern church treat the idea of lamenting? What, if anything, does the church do that's similar? How could a more intentional approach to lamenting help the church?

From the Commentary

David was Israel's lawful king and couldn't remain in Ziklag since it was in enemy territory. It's likely that Achish, the Philistine king, thought that David was still under his authority, but David knew that he must return to his own land and begin to reign over his own people. David was in the habit of seeking the Lord's will when he had to make decisions, either by having Abiathar the priest consult the ephod (1 Sam. 23:9–12) or by asking Gad the prophet to pray to God for a word of wisdom (1 Sam. 22:5).

David was from Judah, so it was logical that he go to live among his own people, but in which city should he reside? God gave him permission to return to Judah and told him to live in Hebron, which was located about twenty-five miles from Ziklag. By moving there, David was back with his own people but still under the shadow of the Philistines. Hebron was important in Jewish history, for near the city was the tomb of Abraham and Sarah, Isaac and Rebekah, and Jacob and Leah. The city was in the inheritance of Caleb, a man of stature in Jewish history (Josh. 14:14). Abigail, one of David's wives, had been married to a Calebite, and David had inherited her property near the wilderness of Maon (1 Sam. 25:2). Hebron was probably the most important city in the southern part of Judah, so David moved there with his men, and they lived in the towns surrounding Hebron. For the first time in ten years, David and his men were no longer fugitives. His men had suffered with him, and now they would reign with him (see 2 Tim. 2:12).

—Be Restored, pages 23–24

5. What does it say about David that he inquired of the Lord about the city he should live in? Why did it matter which city David returned to? What was the symbolic importance of Hebron? Why would God want David in a city so close to the Philistines?

From the Commentary

David was a man with a shepherd's heart who cared about his people (see 2 Sam. 24:17), and one of his first concerns was the fate of Saul and the three sons who died with him. When he asked the leaders of Judah about the burial of the royal family, they told him how the men of Jabesh Gilead had risked their lives to recover the four bodies, burn away the decayed and mutilated flesh, and then bury the bones back at Jabesh (1 Sam. 31:8–13). They remembered how Saul had rescued their city many years before (1 Sam. 11).

Jabesh Gilead was located across the Jordan in the tribe of Gad, and the men who recovered the bodies had to travel northwest and cross the Jordan River to reach Beth Shan, a round trip of perhaps twenty-five miles. It was a courageous endeavor, and David thanked them for their devotion to Saul and to the kingdom of Israel. They had displayed "kindness," and the Lord would show them "kindness and faithfulness" (2 Sam. 2:5–6 NIV). Twenty-five years later, David would disinter the remains of Saul and the sons who died with him and rebury them in their native tribe of Benjamin (2 Sam. 21:12–14).

—*Be Restored*, page 25

6. Review 2 Samuel 2:4–7. Why was it important to collect the bones of Saul and his sons? What did this say about the appreciation these people had for the unpredictable king? What does this teach us about the role of respect for those who've gone before, even if they lived notably imperfect lives?

From the Commentary

"In order to govern," said Napoleon on his deathbed, "the question is not to follow out a more or less valid theory but to build with whatever materials are at hand. The inevitable must be accepted and turned to advantage." If this statement is true, then David was a very effective leader during the seven and a half years he ruled in Hebron. While Joab led the army of Judah, David watched and waited, knowing that the Lord would one day open the way for him to reign as king over all Israel. God called David, not only to be the king of His people, but also their shepherd and spiritual leader. David had to wait on God's timing while patiently enduring the consequences of the selfish ambitions and reckless actions of leaders who were motivated by pride and hatred. David learned to build with the materials at hand and to trust God to use disappointments to the advantage of His people.

The key actor in this drama was Abner, Saul's cousin and the commander of his army (1 Sam. 14:50). It was Abner who brought David to Saul after David killed Goliath (17:55–58), and who with Saul pursued David for ten years (26:5ff.). Abner was rebuked and humiliated by David when he failed to protect the king (26:13–16), and Abner had no special love for David. The people of Israel honored David above Saul, and eventually the nation would learn that David was God's choice as king of Israel. But David already had a commander, Joab, so when David became king, what would happen to Abner?

—Be Restored, pages 29–30

7. Review 2 Samuel 2:8–32. Why did Abner not care for David? What was his response to David's kingship? (See vv. 8–11.) In what ways was Abner only out for his own self-interest? How were his actions similar to the way people sometimes act today in the church when they don't agree with leadership?

From the Commentary

> When Abner made Ish-Bosheth king, he was actually declaring war on David, and he knew it. But by now Abner had all the tribes except Judah behind him, and he felt he could easily defeat David in battle and take over the entire kingdom. Confident of victory, Abner called for a contest between the two armies, to be held at the great cistern about twenty-three miles north of Gibeon.
>
> —Be Restored, page 31

8. Why did Abner believe he could defeat David? What had he missed in his analysis? How was the challenge he called for similar to the one Goliath issued in 1 Samuel 17:8–10?

More to Consider: Polygamy started with Lamech, a descendant of Cain (Gen. 4:19), and was tolerated in Israel, but it was forbidden to Israel's kings (Deut. 17:17). David's family was increasing (1 Chron. 3:1–4), and the king now had a growing harem like any other eastern monarch. David had moved to Hebron with two wives, and now he had six sons by six different wives. Why did David choose to go against the law here? How did his decisions compare to those of his son Solomon? In what ways might this be a case of "like father, like son"?

From the Commentary

It looked as though everything was in good order for a peaceful transition, but there were hidden land mines in the diplomatic field, and they were ready to explode. Ish-Bosheth was still on the throne, and David would have to deal with him and the loyal supporters of the house of Saul. Abner had killed Asahel, and Joab was biding his time until he could avenge his brother's death.

David had sent Joab and some of his men on a raid to secure wealth to help support the kingdom. On his return, when Joab heard that David had received Abner and given him a feast, his anger erupted and he rebuked the king. The key idea in 2 Samuel 3:21–25 is that Saul's general and the man who killed young Asahel had come and gone "in peace" (vv. 21–23), and Joab couldn't understand it. His own heart was still pained at the death of his brother, and Joab couldn't understand his sovereign's policies. Of course, Joab was protecting his own job just as Abner was protecting his, but unlike David, Joab didn't have any faith in what Abner said or did. Joab was certain that Abner's visit had nothing to do with turning the kingdom over to David. The wily general was only spying out the situation and getting ready for an attack.

The text records no reply from David. Joab had never been easy to deal with (2 Sam. 3:39), and the fact that he was a relative made the situation even more difficult. The dynamics of David's family—the multiple wives, the many children, and various relatives in places of authority—created endless problems for the king, and they weren't easy to solve.

—*Be Restored*, pages 36–37

9. Why did David receive Abner and give him a feast? Was David promoting "peace at any price"? Why or why not? In what ways was he demonstrating restraint? How did he illustrate integrity in his dealings with both Abner and Joab?

From the Commentary

If David thought he was weak because of the behavior of his nephews, he should have considered the situation of Ish-Bosheth following the death of Abner. David was at least a great warrior and a gifted leader, while Ish-Bosheth was a mere puppet in the hands of his general, and now the general was dead. The people of the tribes in his kingdom knew that Abner's death meant the end of the reign of their king, and they no doubt expected a swift invasion by David and his army. The common people knew nothing of David's intentions or of his recent meeting with Abner. It was a day of distress for Ish-Bosheth and his people.

The account of Baanah and Rechab reminds us of the Amalekite in 2 Samuel 1, the man who claimed he killed Saul. These two men were minor officers in Abner's army who thought they could earn rewards and promotion from David if they killed Ish-Bosheth and like the Amalekite, they were wrong. The only living heir to Saul's throne was a crippled twelve-year-old boy named Mephibosheth, so if Baanah and Rechab killed the king, the way would be open for David to gain the throne and unite the nation. (We will meet Mephibosheth again in 9:1–13; 16:1–4; 19:24–30; and 21:7–8.)

Their excuse for entering the king's house was to secure grain for their men, and while the king was asleep and unprotected, they killed him. If the murder of Abner was a heinous crime, this murder was even worse, for the man's only "crime" was that he was the son of Saul. He had broken no law and injured no person, and he wasn't given the opportunity to defend himself. His murderers didn't even show respect to his dead body, for they beheaded him so they could take the evidence to David and receive their reward. Even worse, the two murderers told David that the Lord had avenged him.

—*Be Restored*, pages 39–40

10. Review 2 Samuel 4. Why did the two murderers expect a reward from David? What was David's answer to these two? What does this tell us about David's character at this point in his life?

Looking Inward

Take a moment to reflect on all that you've explored thus far in this study of 2 Samuel 1—4 and 1 Chronicles 10:1–12. Review your notes and answers and think about how each of these things matters in your life today.

Tips for Small Groups: To get the most out of this section, form pairs or trios and have group members take turns answering these questions. Be honest and as open as you can in this discussion, but most of all, be encouraging and supportive of others. Be sensitive to those who are going through particularly difficult times and don't press for people to speak if they're uncomfortable doing so.

11. Have you ever taken time to intentionally lament? If you have, describe the circumstances. How has lamenting helped you to honor the past? How has it helped you to be better equipped for the future? If you're a stranger to lamenting, talk about why that might be.

12. When, if ever, have you been tempted to lie to a leader because you were embarrassed by your actions (or lack of action)? What was the result of that lie? How might you have better dealt with the situation?

13. Have you ever backed the wrong leader? What led to your decision to support this person? What had you missed in your analysis of this leader's strengths, abilities, or purpose? How did you recover from this situation?

Going Forward

14. Think of one or two things that you have learned that you'd like to work on in the coming week. Remember that this is all about quality, not quantity. It's better to work on one specific area of life and do it well than to work on many and do poorly (or to be so overwhelmed that you simply don't try).

Do you need to learn how to lament? Be specific. Go back through 2 Samuel 1—4 and 1 Chronicles 10:1–12 and put a star next to the phrase or verse that is most encouraging to you. Consider memorizing this verse.

Real-Life Application Ideas: Arrange a lamentation gathering with your family or small group. Study the concept of lamentation with your family or small group before determining a format for the event. Then use this time to honor those who have gone before, focusing on the wisdom and legacies they've left behind. Lamenting can be a powerful time of cleansing and hope, in addition to the obvious experience of grieving.

Seeking Help

15. Write a prayer below (or simply pray one in silence), inviting God to work on your mind and heart in those areas you've noted in the Going Forward section. Be honest about your desires and fears.

Notes for Small Groups:

- *Look for ways to put into practice the things you wrote in the Going Forward section. Talk with other group members about your ideas and commit to being accountable to one another.*

- *During the coming week, ask the Holy Spirit to continue to reveal truth to you from what you've read and studied.*

- *Before you start the next lesson, read 2 Samuel 5—6 and 1 Chronicles 3:4–8; 11:1–9; 13:5—16:3. For more in-depth lesson preparation, read chapter 3, "David, King of Israel," in* Be Restored.

King of Israel
(2 SAMUEL 5—6; 1 CHRONICLES 3:4–8; 11:1–9; 13:5—16:3)

Before you begin …
- *Pray for the Holy Spirit to reveal truth and wisdom as you go through this lesson.*
- *Read 2 Samuel 5—6 and 1 Chronicles 3:4–8; 11:1–9; 13:5—16:3. This lesson references chapter 3 in* Be Restored. *It will be helpful for you to have your Bible and a copy of the commentary available as you work through this lesson.*

Getting Started

From the Commentary

What a remarkable and varied life David lived! As a shepherd, he killed a lion and a bear, and these victories prepared him to kill the giant Goliath. David served as an attendant to King Saul and became a beloved friend of Saul's son Jonathan. For perhaps ten years, David was an exile in the wilderness of Judea, hiding from Saul and learning to trust the Lord more and more. He had patiently waited for the

Lord to give him the promised throne, and now that time had come. It is through faith and patience that God's people inherit what He has promised (Heb. 6:12), and David had trusted God in the most difficult circumstances.

—*Be Restored,* page 45

1. How did each step in David's journey prepare him for the next one? What challenges did he face by inheriting a divided people? What steps did he take to unite them?

2. Choose one verse or phrase from 2 Samuel 5—6 or 1 Chronicles 3:4–8; 11:1–9; 13:5—16:3 that stands out to you. This could be something you're intrigued by, something that makes you uncomfortable, something that puzzles you, something that resonates with you, or just something you want to examine further. Write that here.

Going Deeper

From the Commentary

> The assassination of Ish-Bosheth left the eleven tribes without a king or even an heir to Saul's throne. Abner was dead, but he had paved the way for David to be made king of all twelve tribes (2 Sam. 3:17–21). The next step was for the leaders of all the tribes to convene at Hebron and crown David king.
>
> —*Be Restored*, page 46

3. How had Abner paved the way for David to be king of all twelve tribes? Why was a single king over all twelve tribes so important to the people of Israel? What challenges did David's rule still face? How does the manner in which the people went about crowning David king compare to the way leaders are chosen in the church today? In the world at large?

More to Consider: Review the qualifications for Israel's king in Deuteronomy 17:14–20. In what ways was David qualified to be king? (See also 2 Sam. 5:2; Ps. 78:70–72; Gen. 49:10.) Is it significant that he was born and raised in Bethlehem? Why or why not?

From the Commentary

The people who gathered at Hebron reminded David that he belonged to the whole nation and not just to the tribe of Judah (2 Sam. 5:1). At the beginning of David's career, the people recognized that God's hand was upon him, for God gave him success in his military exploits. Present at Hebron were representatives from all the tribes, and they enthusiastically gave their allegiance to the new king (1 Chron. 12:23–40). The total number of officers and men is 340,800, all of them loyal to David. The people remained with David for three days and celebrated God's goodness to His people.

—*Be Restored*, page 46

4. In what ways did David belong to the whole nation? How was it significant that even the fighting men of Saul's tribe of Benjamin (1 Chron. 12:29) went to Hebron to acclaim David as king? What do you think was the purpose of the three days of feasting together?

From Today's World

In David's time, the process for determining a new leader was based on a whole host of factors—bloodline, for example—that we don't have to consider today in most countries. But choosing a leader, whether for a nation or a company or a book club, still demands careful attention to what we know of the potential leader's character. In this day and age when everything is chronicled online, there's little hiding any mistakes made or character flaws. This is why it's often so difficult for a nation, or a church, to choose a new leader.

5. What are the most important characteristics in choosing a leader, regardless of the organization or group that's being led? How does the specific nature of the organization or group determine additional positive qualities for a leader? Why is the choice of a leader so important? What can we learn from David's character (both good and bad) that can help us make good choices?

From the Commentary

The foundation of the Jewish nation was God's covenant with His people as expressed in the law of Moses, especially Deuteronomy 27—30 and Leviticus 26. If the king and the people obeyed God's will, He would bless and care for them; but if they disobeyed and worshipped false gods, He would discipline them. Each new king was required to affirm the supremacy and authority of God's law, promise to obey it, and even make a copy of it for his own personal use (Deut. 17:18–20). David entered into a covenant with the Lord and the people, agreeing to uphold and obey God's law and to rule in the fear of the Lord (see 1 Sam. 10:17–25; 2 Kings 11:17).

When David was a teenager, Samuel had anointed him privately (1 Sam. 16:13), and the elders of the tribe of Judah had anointed him when he became their king at thirty years of age (2 Sam. 2:4). But now the elders of the whole nation anointed David and proclaimed him as their king. David was not an amateur, but a seasoned warrior and a gifted leader who obviously had the blessing of the Lord on his life and ministry. After experiencing years of turbulence and division, the nation at last had a king who was God's choice and the people's choice.

—*Be Restored*, page 47

6. What does the appointment of David as king tell us about how God prepares His leaders? What does it say about the challenges God's leaders face on their journey toward leadership? During their rule? What lessons can we apply from this to how we deal with our own leaders?

From the Commentary

Abner and Ish-Bosheth had established their capital at
Mahanaim (2 Sam. 2:8), over the Jordan River on the
boundary of Gad and Manasseh, while David's capital was
at Hebron in the tribe of Judah. But neither city was suitable
for a new ruler who was seeking to unify the nation and
make a new beginning. David wisely chose as his capital
the Jebusite city of Jerusalem on the border of Benjamin
(Saul's tribe) and Judah (David's tribe). Jerusalem had never
belonged to any of the tribes, so nobody could accuse David
of playing favorites in setting up his new capital.

Political considerations were important, but so was security,
and the topography of Jerusalem made it an ideal capital city.
Built on a rocky hill and surrounded on three sides by valleys
and hills, the city was vulnerable only on the north side. The
Valley of Hinnom lay on the south, the Kidron Valley on the
east, and the Tyropean Valley on the west. "Beautiful for situation, the joy of the whole earth, is mount Zion, on the sides
of the north, the city of the great King" (Ps. 48:2). "Out of
Zion, the perfection of beauty, God hath shined" (Ps. 50:2).
The Jewish people have always loved the city of Jerusalem,
and today it is revered by Jews, Christians, and Muslims.

—*Be Restored*, pages 47–48

7. Review 2 Samuel 5:6–10 and 1 Chronicles 11:4–9. Why was the location of
the city so important? Why is it significant that Jerusalem never belonged to any
of the tribes? Read Psalm 87. What does this passage tell us about Jerusalem?

More to Consider: The word "Millo" (2 Sam. 5:9; "terraces" in NIV) means "fullness" and refers to a stone embankment that was built on the southeastern side of the mount to support additional buildings and a wall. Archaeologists have uncovered what they call "a stepped-stone structure," about fifteen hundred feet long and nine hundred feet wide, that was a supporting terrace for other structures, and they assume this was the Millo. Both Solomon and King Hezekiah strengthened this part of Mount Zion (1 Kings 9:15, 24; 11:27; 2 Chron. 32:5). How is the mention of this structure evidence of God's blessing on David? In what ways does the eventual splendor of Jerusalem and the temple speak to God's blessing on His people? How do we often misinterpret this kind of blessing today?

From the Commentary

The mention of David's palace and his alliance with Hiram offered the writer opportunity to mention David's family, the "house" that the Lord was building for him (Ps. 127). Deuteronomy 17:17 prohibited Israel's king from taking many wives, but David seems to have ignored this law, as did Solomon after him (1 Kings 11:1–4). At least one of David's wives was a princess (2 Sam. 3:3), which suggests that the marriage was for the sake of political alliance; and no doubt there were other similar marriages. This was one way to cement good relationships with other nations.

—*Be Restored*, page 50

8. Why did David seemingly ignore the law about taking many wives? What does this tell us about David's personality? About his regard for the law? What risks was he taking by marrying many wives? What risks would he have taken had he not?

From the Commentary

As long as David was minding his own business in Hebron, the Philistines thought he was still one of their vassals; but when he became king of the whole nation of Israel, the Philistines knew he was their enemy, and they attacked him. It's probable that these attacks occurred before David relocated in Jerusalem, because he and his men went down to "the stronghold" (2 Sam. 5:17 NKJV), the wilderness area where he had lived in the days when Saul was out to kill him (1 Sam. 22:4; 23:13–14). David got word of the approaching Philistine army, quickly maneuvered his soldiers, and met the invaders in the valley of Rephaim, just a short distance from Jerusalem.

As he had done before, David sought the mind of the Lord in planning his attack, probably by using the Urim and Thummim; or he may have had the prophet Gad seek the Lord's will. Assured by the Lord that He would give Israel victory, David met the Philistines two miles southwest of Jerusalem, and he forced them to retreat. They left the field so quickly that they left their idols behind, and David and his men burned them. The Philistines were sure the presence of their gods would assure them victory, but they were wrong. David gave God all the glory and called the place Baal-perazim, which means "the Lord who breaks out."

—*Be Restored*, page 51

9. How did David seek the Lord's guidance before facing the Philistines? What are the battles that the church faces today? How does the modern church seek God's guidance before going into battle?

From the Commentary

The ark of the covenant was to be kept in the Holy of Holies of the tabernacle, for it symbolized the glorious throne of God (Ps. 80:1; 99:1 NIV); but for over seventy-five years, the ark had been absent from the divine sanctuary at Shiloh. The Philistines captured the ark when Eli was judge (1 Sam. 4) and then returned it to the Jews because the Lord sent judgment on the Philistines. First the ark was sent to Beth-Shemesh and then was taken to Kiriath Jearim and guarded in the house of Abinadab (1 Sam 5:1—7:1). During the reign of David, there were two high priests, Zadok and

Ahimelech (2 Sam. 8:17), and it's possible that one served at the sanctuary, which was in Shiloh, and then moved to Gibeon (2 Chron. 1:1–6), while the other ministered at court in Jerusalem. David pitched a tent for the ark in the city of David, but the furnishings in the tabernacle weren't moved to Jerusalem until after Solomon completed the temple (1 Kings 8:1–4; 2 Chron. 5:1–5).

—Be Restored, pages 52–53

10. Why did David want the ark in Jerusalem? What were his personal reasons? What were the political reasons? His hopes weren't fully realized until Solomon completed the temple. What does this say about how David's plans for the ark and God's plans lined up?

Looking Inward

Take a moment to reflect on all that you've explored thus far in this study of 2 Samuel 5—6 and 1 Chronicles 3:4–8; 11:1–9; 13:5—16:3. Review your notes and answers and think about how each of these things matters in your life today.

Tips for Small Groups: To get the most out of this section, form pairs or trios and have group members take turns answering these questions. Be honest and as open as you can in this discussion, but most of all, be encouraging and supportive of others. Be sensitive to those who are going through particularly difficult times and don't press for people to speak if they're uncomfortable doing so.

11. Can you look back on previous challenges and see them as stepping-stones to where you are in your faith today? If so, explain. How does God use each chapter of our stories to bring us closer to Him and in line with His will?

12. Are you a leader in any capacity? If so, what are some ways God has prepared you to lead? What are some areas in which you still need development to become a strong leader? Where does God's Word fit into that plan for growing as a leader?

13. David sought God's guidance before many of his decisions. How often do you seek God's guidance before making a decision? How do you go about doing this? What are some practical ways to seek God?

Going Forward

14. Think of one or two things that you have learned that you'd like to work on in the coming week. Remember that this is all about quality, not quantity. It's better to work on one specific area of life and do it well than to work on many and do poorly (or to be so overwhelmed that you simply don't try).

Do you want to make a decision in line with being a godly leader? Be specific. Go back through 2 Samuel 5—6 and 1 Chronicles 3:4–8; 11:1–9; 13:5—16:3 and put a star next to the phrase or verse that is most encouraging to you. Consider memorizing this verse.

Real-Life Application Ideas: Before the next workweek starts, take time to consider God's heart in all the big decisions you have coming your way. This could include workplace decisions, family decisions, or financial decisions. Then take advantage of all the resources you have available to discover God's will, including the Bible, Bible study resources, the wise counsel of friends, and, of course, prayer. Establish this as a regular "before the week begins" practice to grow closer to God while making better decisions in the process.

Seeking Help

15. Write a prayer below (or simply pray one in silence), inviting God to work on your mind and heart in those areas you've noted in the Going Forward section. Be honest about your desires and fears.

Notes for Small Groups:
- *Look for ways to put into practice the things you wrote in the Going Forward section. Talk with other group members about your ideas and commit to being accountable to one another.*
- *During the coming week, ask the Holy Spirit to continue to reveal truth to you from what you've read and studied.*
- *Before you start the next lesson, read 2 Samuel 7—10 and 1 Chronicles 17—19. For more in-depth lesson preparation, read chapter 4, "David's Dynasty, Kindness, and Conquests," in* Be Restored.

Dynasty

(2 SAMUEL 7—10; 1 CHRONICLES 17—19)

Before you begin ...

- *Pray for the Holy Spirit to reveal truth and wisdom as you go through this lesson.*
- *Read 2 Samuel 7—10 and 1 Chronicles 17—19. This lesson references chapter 4 in* Be Restored. *It will be helpful for you to have your Bible and a copy of the commentary available as you work through this lesson.*

Getting Started

From the Commentary

In 2 Samuel 7—10, we see King David involved in four important activities: accepting God's will (chap. 7), fighting God's battles (chap. 8), sharing God's kindness (chap. 9), and defending God's honor (chap. 10). However, these activities were nothing new to David, for even before he was crowned king of all Israel, he had served the Lord and the people in these ways. Wearing a crown and sitting on a throne didn't change David, for in his character and conduct, he had lived like a king all his young life.

How tragic that from chapter 11 on, we see David disobeying the Lord and suffering the painful consequences of his sins.

—*Be Restored*, page 61

1. Andrew Bonar said, "We must be as watchful after the victory as before the battle." How is this statement true in David's story? How is this true in the church today? What are the dangers of focusing too much on our victories?

2. Choose one verse or phrase from 2 Samuel 7—10 or 1 Chronicles 17—19 that stands out to you. This could be something you're intrigued by, something that makes you uncomfortable, something that puzzles you, something that resonates with you, or just something you want to examine further. Write that here.

Going Deeper

From the Commentary

In the ancient world, what did kings do when they had no wars to fight? Nebuchadnezzar surveyed his city and boasted, "Is not this great Babylon, that I have built?" (Dan. 4:30). Solomon collected wealth and wives, entertained foreign guests, and wrote books, while Hezekiah seems to have supervised scholars who copied and preserved the Scriptures (Prov. 25:1). But it appears from 2 Samuel 7:1–3 that in David's leisure hours, the king thought about the Lord and conferred with his chaplain, Nathan, about improving the spiritual condition of the kingdom of Israel. David wasn't simply a ruler; he was a shepherd with a heart concern for his people. In rest, he thought of work he could do, and in success he thought of God and His goodness to him.

—*Be Restored*, page 62

3. In a later chapter, we'll discover that David spent his leisure time doing other things, but in 2 Samuel 7, he seemed focused on a very important theme: spiritual growth. What sorts of things might he have pondered during this season of his life? How does a leader go about improving the spiritual condition of a nation? Or even of a family?

From the Commentary

> That David wanted to build a house for the Lord doesn't surprise us, because David was a man after God's own heart and longed to honor the Lord in every possible way. During his years of exile, David had vowed to the Lord that he would build Him a temple (Ps. 132:1–5), and his bringing the ark to Jerusalem was surely the first step toward fulfilling that vow. Now it troubled David that he was living in a comfortable stone house with cedar paneling while God's throne was in a tent, and he shared his burden with Nathan.
>
> —*Be Restored*, page 62

4. We'll see the phrase "David was a man after God's own heart" more than a few times in this study. How does it apply in David's desire to build God's temple in Jerusalem? Why would David be troubled by the apparent disparity between his living conditions and God's? What was good about David's desire? What, if anything, might have been misplaced about it?

More to Consider: This is the first appearance of Nathan in Scripture. Gad had been David's prophet during his exile (1 Sam. 22:5), and after David's coronation, Gad didn't pass from the scene (2 Sam. 24:1–18). In fact, he and Nathan worked together keeping the official records (1 Chron. 29:29) and organizing the worship (2 Chron. 29:25), but Nathan seems to have been the prophetic voice of God to David during his reign. Why might God have chosen someone new to speak to David at this point in his life? (See 2 Sam. 12; 1 Kings 1:11ff.). What did Nathan mean when he told David to do what was in his heart? Did this mean his desires were actually God's desires? Why or why not? How do we sort through all the voices speaking to us about what we should do? Who are our Nathans?

From Today's World

David had big plans for building a "home" for God. Though his plans were delayed (and later completed by his son Solomon), his intent was pure. Today there are many churches that are struggling to keep their doors open. But there are also churches that continue to grow, with no end in sight to how big they can become. This brings into play the age-old church questions of "When is it time to build?" and "When is it time to find a bigger building?" These are not small questions, as the infrastructure of a church can be a tricky thing to maintain in a world where membership may be fickle.

5. What are the greatest challenges facing today's church when it comes to buildings and facilities? How can a church budget determine the long-term success or failure of a congregation? What are the risks of building too soon or asking too much of a congregation? What are the risks of not

acting soon enough? What does David's temple-building dream say to us today about God's timing in such things?

From the Commentary

> The foundation for God's purposes and dealings with the people of Israel is His covenant with Abraham (Gen. 12:1–3; 15:1–15). God chose Abraham by His grace and promised him a land, a great name, multiplied descendants, and His blessing and protection. He also promised that the whole world would be blessed through Abraham's seed, and this refers to Jesus Christ (Gal. 3:1–16). God called Israel to be the human channel through which His Son and His Word would come to the world. God's covenant with David builds on this covenant with Abraham, for it speaks about the nation, the land, and the Messiah.
>
> —*Be Restored*, pages 63–64

6. How did God's covenant with David build on the covenant with Abraham? What did this covenant mean to Israel? What promises did God make to His people in the Davidic covenant?

From the Commentary

God's first announcement of the coming of the Savior was given in Genesis 3:15, informing us that the Savior would be a human being and not an angel. Genesis 12:3 tells us that He would be a Jew who would bless the whole world, and Genesis 49:10 that He would come through the tribe of Judah. In this covenant, God announced to David that the Messiah would come through his family, and Micah 5:2 prophesied that He would be born in Bethlehem, the city of David (see Matt. 2:6). No wonder the king was so elated when he learned that the Messiah would be known as "the son of David" (Matt. 1:1)!

In 2 Samuel 7:10–16, the Lord speaks about Solomon as well as about the Savior, who is "greater than Solomon" (Matt. 12:42). Solomon would build the temple David longed to build, but his reign would end; however, the reign of the Messiah would go on forever. David would have a house forever (2 Sam. 7:25, 29), a kingdom forever (v. 16), and a throne forever (vv. 13, 16), and would glorify God's name forever (v. 26).

—*Be Restored*, page 65

7. Why was it significant that the Messiah would come through the line of David? What did this mean to David's legacy? What did it say about God's relationship with David? Why is Solomon referenced in this passage? Why make the contrast between Solomon and the coming Messiah?

From the Commentary

We have already noted that there is a church today because God used David's family to bring the Savior into the world, and there is a future for Israel because God gave David a throne forever. The way that David responded to this great word from God is a good example for us to follow today. He humbled himself before the Lord and, at least ten times, called himself the servant of God. Servants usually stand at attention and wait for orders, but David sat before the Lord. The covenant God gave David was unconditional; all David had to do was accept it and let God work. Like a little child speaking to a loving parent, the king called himself "David" (2 Sam. 7:20), and he poured out his heart to the Lord.

First, he focused on *the present* as he gave praise for the mercies God bestowed on him (vv. 18–21).

In verses 22–24, David looked at *the past* and God's amazing grace toward Israel.

The third part of David's prayer and praise (vv. 25–29) looked to *the future* as revealed in the covenant just delivered to the king.

—*Be Restored*, pages 66–67

8. Review 2 Samuel 7:18–29. How is David's response to God a good example for us today? What is the value of reflecting on the present in regard to our relationship with God? What role can the past play in helping us grow closer to God? How can a focus on the future help God's people?

More to Consider: David's victories enriched the treasury of the Lord so that the material was available for Solomon to build the temple (2 Sam. 8:11–13; 1 Chron. 22). How does the way David fought battles for God compare to the way the church today fights God's battles? (See John 18:36–38; 2 Cor. 10:3–6; Eph. 6:14–18.) What is the lost territory that the Lord wants us to reclaim today?

From the Commentary

"The kindness of God" is one of two themes in 2 Samuel 9 (vv. 1, 3, 7), and it means the mercy and favor of the Lord to undeserving people. Paul saw the kindness of God in the coming of Jesus Christ and His work on the cross (Titus 3:1–7; Eph. 2:1–9), and we see in David's dealings with Mephibosheth a picture of God's kindness to lost sinners. David had promised both Saul and Jonathan that he would not exterminate their descendants when he became king (1 Sam. 20:12–17, 42; 24:21), and in the case of Jonathan's son Mephibosheth, David not only kept his promise but went above and beyond the call of duty.

The second major theme is the kingship of David. The name "David" is used by itself five times in the chapter; eleven times he's called "the king," and once, the two are united in "King David" (2 Sam. 9:5). Nobody in all Israel except David could have shown this kindness to Mephibosheth, because David was the king. He had inherited all that had belonged to King Saul (12:8) and could dispose of it as he saw fit.

—*Be Restored*, page 72

9. Review 2 Samuel 9:1–13. How is David's treatment of Mephibosheth similar to the way Jesus Christ has treated us? Why did David deal kindly with Mephibosheth? What might it have been like for Mephibosheth when he first heard that David had summoned him? What might it have been like for him to eat meals every day with David's sons?

From the Commentary

Once again, David wanted to show kindness, but this time his attempt led to war instead of peace. His overtures to his neighbor were misunderstood, and David had to defend his own honor as well as the honor of the Lord and His people.

David indeed was a man of war and fought the battles of the Lord, and the Lord was with him to give him victory. He extended the Israelite empire to the River of Egypt on the south, to the Euphrates River on the north, and on the east he conquered Edom, Moab, and Ammon, and on the north defeated the Arameans and the Syrians, including Hamath. Because of God's gifts and help, David undoubtedly became Israel's greatest king and greatest military genius. He was blessed with courageous men like Joab and Abishai, plus his mighty men (2 Sam. 23; 1 Chron. 11:10–47).

—*Be Restored*, pages 75, 77

10. Review 2 Samuel 10 and 1 Chronicles 19. Why did David have to fight so many battles? How did he accomplish this? Why wouldn't God simply give him the land or protect him from enemy nations? How did the victory over another nation help to tell the story of God's plan for His people?

Looking Inward

Take a moment to reflect on all that you've explored thus far in this study of 2 Samuel 7—10 and 1 Chronicles 17—19. Review your notes and answers and think about how each of these things matters in your life today.

Tips for Small Groups: To get the most out of this section, form pairs or trios and have group members take turns answering these questions. Be honest and as open as you can in this discussion, but most of all, be encouraging and supportive of others. Be sensitive to those who are going through particularly difficult times and don't press for people to speak if they're uncomfortable doing so.

11. What are some ways in which you deliberately work on your spiritual condition? Is it easy to make time for this? Why or why not? How can you become more diligent in building your spiritual identity?

12. Covenants were important to the Israelites because they came with promises for future success. Do you see your relationship with God as a covenant? If so, what are the promises that define the relationship? How are these promises similar and dissimilar to the covenants the Israelites knew?

13. How much attention do you give to the past when working on your faith life? How much consideration do you give the future? The present? How do you manage all three as you pursue closeness with God?

Going Forward

14. Think of one or two things that you have learned that you'd like to work on in the coming week. Remember that this is all about quality, not quantity. It's better to work on one specific area of life and do it well than to work on many and do poorly (or to be so overwhelmed that you simply don't try).

Do you want to live with gratitude for the covenant God has made with His people, including you? Be specific. Go back through 2 Samuel 7—10 and 1 Chronicles 17—19 and put a star next to the phrase or verse that is most encouraging to you. Consider memorizing this verse.

Real-Life Application Ideas: This week, consider any battles you're facing in life. Perhaps you have some challenges at work or within your family. David trusted God to help guide him in his battles. What would it look like for you to do the same? In Old Testament times, war was often unavoidable. But today, our battles can be won without lifting a weapon. What would it look like to show kindness rather than mount an attack? How can Jesus' example of sacrifice guide you as you meet your opponent on the "battlefield"? Spend lots of time in prayer asking God to help guide you not toward victory that exalts you but victory that honors Him. That's the true measure of victory, even if it appears we've lost according to the world.

Seeking Help

15. Write a prayer below (or simply pray one in silence), inviting God to work on your mind and heart in those areas you've noted in the Going Forward section. Be honest about your desires and fears.

Notes for Small Groups:

- *Look for ways to put into practice the things you wrote in the Going Forward section. Talk with other group members about your ideas and commit to being accountable to one another.*

- *During the coming week, ask the Holy Spirit to continue to reveal truth to you from what you've read and studied.*

- *Before you start the next lesson, read 2 Samuel 11—14. For more in-depth lesson preparation, read chapters 5 and 6, "David's Disobedience, Deception, and Discipline" and "David's Unruly Sons," in* Be Restored.

Disobedience
(2 SAMUEL 11—14)

Before you begin ...
- *Pray for the Holy Spirit to reveal truth and wisdom as you go through this lesson.*
- *Read 2 Samuel 11—14. This lesson references chapters 5 and 6 in* Be Restored. *It will be helpful for you to have your Bible and a copy of the commentary available as you work through this lesson.*

Getting Started

From the Commentary

The account of David's sins is given against the background of Joab's siege of Rabbah, the key city of the Ammonites (2 Sam. 11:1, 16–17; 1 Chron. 20:1–3). The Ammonite army had fled to the walled city of Rabbah (2 Sam. 10:14), and Joab and the Israel troops were giving the people time to run out of food and water, and then they would attack. David sent Joab and the troops to lay siege to Rabbah, but he himself remained in

Jerusalem. It was probably April or May and the winter rains had stopped and the weather was getting warmer. Chronologists calculate that David was about fifty years old at this time. It's true that David had been advised by his leaders not to engage actively in warfare (2 Sam. 21:15–17), but he could have been with his troops to help develop the strategy and give moral leadership.

—*Be Restored*, page 82

1. Review 2 Samuel 11:1–2. What is idleness? How did idleness contribute to David's sin? What should he have been doing during this time? How is idleness a challenge for us in the church today?

More to Consider: When David laid aside his armor, he took the first step toward moral defeat. How does this same principle apply to believers today? (See Eph. 6:10–18.) What happens when we set aside the helmet of salvation, the breastplate of righteousness, the belt of truth, the sword of the Spirit, and the shield of faith?

2. Choose one verse or phrase from 2 Samuel 11—14 that stands out to you. This could be something you're intrigued by, something that makes you uncomfortable, something that puzzles you, something that resonates with you, or just something you want to examine further. Write that here.

Going Deeper

From the Commentary

> A man can't be blamed if a beautiful woman comes into his line of vision, but if the man deliberately lingers for a second look in order to feed his lust, he's asking for trouble. "You heard that it was said, You shall not commit adultery," said Jesus. "But as for myself, I am saying to you, Everyone who is looking at a woman in order to indulge his sexual passion for her, has already committed adultery with her in his heart" (Matt. 5:27–28 WUEST). When David paused and took that longer second look, his imagination went to work and started to conceive sin. That would have been a good time to turn away decisively and leave the roof of his palace for a much safer place. When Joseph faced a similar temptation, he fled from the scene (Gen. 39:11–13). "Watch and pray, lest you enter

into temptation. The spirit indeed is willing, but the flesh is weak" (Matt. 26:41 NKJV).

—*Be Restored*, page 83

3. How did David tempt himself? What role did his imagination play in this temptation? What does this tell us about the risks of letting our imaginations run wild? How can we look to God to help us in situations similar to David's?

From the Commentary

Did Bathsheba even know why David wanted her? If so, didn't she stop to consider that, having just finished her monthly period (2 Sam. 11:2), she was ripe for conception? Maybe she *wanted* to have a baby by the king! First Kings 1 indicates that Bathsheba may have been luring the king. "Did the young wife construct the situation?" asks Professor E. M. Blaiklock. "There is more than suspicion that she spread the net into which David so promptly fell." Perhaps she thought David had news from the front about her husband; but it wasn't the king's job to deliver military announcements. Did she miss her husband's love and take her purification bath in public as a deliberate invitation to any man who happened to be watching? If she refused David's requests, would he punish her husband? (That happened anyway!)

No Jewish citizen had to obey a king who himself was disobeying God's law, for the king covenanted with God and the people to submit to the divine law. Did she think that submitting to David would put into her hands a weapon that might help her in the future, especially if her husband were killed in battle? We can ask these questions and many more, but we can't easily answer them. The biblical text doesn't tell us and educated guesses aren't much help.

—*Be Restored*, page 85

4. Read Proverbs 6:20–29. How does this passage apply to David's sin? If the punishment for adultery was death, why didn't David and Bathsheba suffer this consequence? What did David suffer for his sins? (See 2 Sam. 13; 16:22; 18:14–15; 1 Kings 2:25.) Why this kind of punishment?

From the Commentary

> David was breaking the Ten Commandments one by one.
> He coveted his neighbor's wife and committed adultery
> with her, and now he would bear false witness against
> his neighbor and order him to be killed. David thought
> he was deceiving everybody, but he was deceiving only
> himself. He thought he could escape guilt when, all the
> while, he was adding to his guilt, and he could not escape
> God's judgment. "He who covers his sins will not pros-
> per" (Prov. 28:13 NKJV).
>
> —*Be Restored*, page 87

5. How could someone who had committed so many sins be referred to
as a "man after God's own heart"? Why did he choose deception when he
knew God was aware of everything he did? Why is it so tempting to think
we can get away with sin?

From the Commentary

Nathan had the privilege of delivering the message about God's covenant with David and his descendants (2 Sam. 7), but now the prophet had to perform spiritual surgery and confront the king about his sins. David had been covering his sins for at least six months, and Bathsheba's baby was about to be born. It wasn't an easy task the Lord had given Nathan, but it's obvious that he prepared carefully for his encounter with the guilty king.

In telling a story about the crime of another, Nathan prepared David for dealing with his own sins, and it's possible that David thought Nathan was presenting him with an actual case from the local court. Nathan was catching David off guard and could study the king's response and better know what to do next. Since David had been a shepherd himself, he would pay close attention to a story about the theft of an innocent lamb, and as king, he was obligated to see that poor families were given justice.

God directed Nathan to choose his words carefully so that they would remind David of what he had said and done. The prophet said that the ewe lamb "did eat of his [the poor man's] own meat, and drank of his own cup, and lay in his bosom" (2 Sam. 12:3). This should have reminded David of Uriah's speech in 11:11: "Shall I then go to my house to eat and drink, and to lie with my wife?" (NKJV). But it wasn't until Nathan told about the rich man stealing and killing the lamb that David showed any response, and then he was angry at another man's sins.

(See 1 Sam. 25:13, 22, 33 for another example of David's anger.) David didn't seem to realize that he was the rich man, Uriah was the poor man, and Bathsheba was the ewe lamb he had stolen. The traveler whom the rich man fed represents the temptation and lust that visited David on the roof and then controlled him. If we open the door, sin comes in as a guest but soon becomes the master. (See Gen. 4:6–7.)

—*Be Restored*, pages 88–89

6. Review 2 Samuel 12:1–14. Why did God choose to use Nathan to speak to David's sins? Why wouldn't God speak directly to David, considering how uniquely close their relationship was? What was David's initial response to Nathan's confrontation? How is this similar to the way we often respond to being caught in sin today?

More to Consider: David's week of fasting and prayer for the baby showed his faith in the Lord and his love for Bathsheba and her little son. Very few Middle Eastern monarchs would have shed a tear or expressed a sentence of sorrow if a baby died who had been born to one of the harem wives. In spite of his many sins, David was still a tender shepherd; he had not been "hardened by sin's deceitfulness" (Heb. 3:13). Read Genesis 35:1–2; 41:14; Exodus 19:10; Leviticus 14:8–9; Jeremiah 52:33; and Revelation 3:18. How do these verses speak to the concept of "washing" and "changing clothes" that David practiced in this situation? What do these actions symbolize? What do they teach us for our lives today?

From the Commentary

No matter how devastated the chastening hand of our loving Father makes us feel, there is comfort available from the Lord (see Isa. 40:1–2, 9–11, 28–31). Before her son died, God called Bathsheba "Uriah's wife" (2 Sam. 12:15), possibly because that's who she was when the boy was conceived; but in verse 24, she is David's wife, which suggests that, like David, she is also making a new beginning. What an evidence of God's grace that "the wife of Uriah" is mentioned in the genealogy of the Messiah (Matt. 1:6), along with Tamar (Matt. 1:3; Gen. 38) and Rahab and Ruth (Matt. 1:5; Josh. 2; 6:22–25; Ruth 1; 4; Deut. 23:3).

At least nine months are compressed into 2 Samuel 12:24–25, nine months of God's grace and tender mercy.

It was God who caused the conception to occur and who saw to it that the baby would have the genetic structure that he would need to accomplish God's will (Ps. 139:13–16). In a very special way, "the Lord loved him" and even gave Solomon ("peaceable") a special name, "Jedidiah"—"loved by the Lord." Since "David" means "beloved," father and son were bound together by similar names. God had told David that this son would be born and that he would build the temple (2 Sam. 7:12–13; 1 Chron. 22:6–10), and He kept His promise.

—*Be Restored*, page 94

7. Review 2 Samuel 12:24–25. Why does David's story have such an emphasis on comfort? What does this teach us about God's love for us no matter what our choices? What does it tell us about God's character? How did God use comfort to help David and Bathsheba secure a better future? How does He do that for us today?

From the Commentary

We have seen in the first ten chapters of 2 Samuel how God empowered David to defeat Israel's enemies and establish and expand the kingdom. Then David committed the sins of adultery, murder, and deception (2 Sam. 11—12), and the rest of the book describes David wrestling with problems caused by his own children. His days are dark and disappointing, but he still depends on the Lord, and the Lord enables him to overcome and prepare the nations for the reign of his son Solomon. What life does to us depends on what life finds in us, and in David was a muscular faith in the living God.

Absalom is the chief actor in this part of the drama, for it was Absalom who helped to turn the drama into a tragedy. The three heirs to David's throne were Amnon, David's firstborn, Absalom, his third son, and Adonijah, who was born fourth (1 Chron. 3:1–2). God had warned David that the sword would not depart from his own household (2 Sam. 12:10), and Absalom (which means "peaceful") was the first to take up that sword. David's judgment against the rich man in Nathan's story was, "He shall restore the lamb fourfold" (12:6), and that judgment fell upon David's own head. Bathsheba's baby died; Absalom killed Amnon for raping Tamar; Joab killed Absalom during the battle of Mount Ephraim; and Adonijah was slain for trying to usurp the throne from Solomon (1 Kings 2:12–25).

—*Be Restored*, page 99

8. In what ways did David discover the painful consequences of his sin through his family members? What example had David set for his sons by behaving as he had with Bathsheba and Uriah? What message is there for us today in this painful chapter in David's story?

From the Commentary

Amnon thought he loved Tamar. First, he was distressed over her (2 Sam. 13:1–2), and then he became ill longing for her (v. 2) even to the point of looking haggard (v. 4). But after he committed the shameful act, he hated Tamar vehemently and wanted to get rid of her (v. 15). True love would never violate another person's body just to satisfy selfish appetites, nor would true love try to persuade someone to disobey the law of God. In his sensual cravings, Amnon confused lust with love and didn't realize that there is a fine line between selfish love (lust) and hatred. Before he sinned, he wanted Tamar all to himself, but after he sinned, he couldn't get rid of her fast enough.

Sexual sins usually produce that kind of emotional damage. When you treat other people like things to be used, you end up throwing them aside like broken toys or old clothes. The word "woman" is not in the Hebrew text of verse 17, so Amnon was saying, "Throw this thing out!" This explains why Tamar accused Amnon of being even more cruel by casting her aside than by raping her. Having lost her virginity, Tamar was not a good prospect for marriage, and she could no longer reside in the apartments with the virgins. Where would she go? Who would take her in? Who would even want her? How could she prove that Amnon was the aggressor and that she hadn't seduced him?

—*Be Restored*, page 102

9. Review 2 Samuel 13:1–22. How was Amnon's sin like his father's sin? Why does the Old Testament include brutal stories such as this one? What does this kind of story teach us about the depravity of humans? What does it teach us about God's sovereignty?

From the Commentary

Tamar may have said that she was going to the king to tell him what happened, but her brother suggested that she wait. Why? Because Absalom's cunning brain was already at work on a scheme that would accomplish three purposes: avenge Tamar, get rid of Amnon, and put himself next in line for the throne. His statement "He's your brother" (2 Sam. 13:20 NKJV) means, "If it were any other man, I would avenge you immediately; but since it's your brother, I'll have to be patient and wait for an opportunity."

There is no record that Absalom was repentant and sought his father's forgiveness, or that he visited the temple and offered the required sacrifices. Father and son were together again, but it was a fragile truce and not a real peace. Absalom still had his hidden agenda and was determined to seize David's throne. Now that the prince was free, he could be visible in the city and enjoy the adulation of the crowds, while at the same time quietly organizing his sympathizers for the coming rebellion. David was about to lose his throne and crown, his concubines, his trusted adviser Ahithophel, and ultimately his son Absalom. It would be the darkest hour in David's life.

—*Be Restored*, pages 103, 111

10. Why did Absalom decide to avenge Tamar himself? David was furious when he heard about Tamar (2 Sam. 13:21), but he didn't punish Amnon or help Tamar. What does that say about him? God had promised that David would pay a price through his children; does that mean this episode was God's fault? Explain.

Looking Inward

Take a moment to reflect on all that you've explored thus far in this study of 2 Samuel 11—14. Review your notes and answers and think about how each of these things matters in your life today.

Tips for Small Groups: To get the most out of this section, form pairs or trios and have group members take turns answering these questions. Be honest and as open as you can in this discussion, but most of all, be encouraging and supportive of others. Be sensitive to those who are going through particularly difficult times and don't press for people to speak if they're uncomfortable doing so.

11. Think of a time when your imagination got you into trouble. What led to that result? How might you have better dealt with the situation so you wouldn't have given in to temptation? Think of a time when your imagination helped you make a good decision. What's the difference between these two scenarios?

12. Despite David's significant failures as a man and a father, he was still "a man after God's own heart." How do you make sense of that? Would you

consider yourself someone who's "after God's own heart"? If so, what does that mean to you? If not, what's holding you back?

13. Describe a time when you wanted to get revenge on someone. What prompted that desire? Was it warranted? If you did take revenge, how did that affect you? If you didn't, how did you resolve that desire?

Going Forward

14. Think of one or two things that you have learned that you'd like to work on in the coming week. Remember that this is all about quality, not quantity. It's better to work on one specific area of life and do it well than to work on many and do poorly (or to be so overwhelmed that you simply don't try).

Do you want to learn what it means to be someone after God's own heart? Be specific. Go back through 2 Samuel 11—14 and put a star next to the phrase or verse that is most encouraging to you. Consider memorizing this verse.

Real-Life Application Ideas: This week, consider times in your life when you felt wronged or when someone you cared about was wronged and you wanted to take revenge on the perpetrator. Reexamine what prompted your desire for revenge. What was appropriate about your anger? What was inappropriate? Did you turn to God in those situations? If you did, what was His answer to you? If you didn't, why didn't you? Then spend time each day this week in prayer asking God to give you wisdom whenever you face a situation that might cause you to feel vengeful, so you might act according to God's will and not your own.

Seeking Help

15. Write a prayer below (or simply pray one in silence), inviting God to work on your mind and heart in those areas you've noted in the Going Forward section. Be honest about your desires and fears.

Notes for Small Groups:

- *Look for ways to put into practice the things you wrote in the Going Forward section. Talk with other group members about your ideas and commit to being accountable to one another.*

- *During the coming week, ask the Holy Spirit to continue to reveal truth to you from what you've read and studied.*

- *Before you start the next lesson, read 2 Samuel 15:1— 16:14. For more in-depth lesson preparation, read chapter 7, "David's Escape to the Wilderness," in* Be Restored.

Escape
(2 SAMUEL 15:1—16:14)

Before you begin ...
- *Pray for the Holy Spirit to reveal truth and wisdom as you go through this lesson.*
- *Read 2 Samuel 15:1—16:14. This lesson references chapter 7 in* Be Restored. *It will be helpful for you to have your Bible and a copy of the commentary available as you work through this lesson.*

Getting Started

From the Commentary

It's one thing to experience God's power when you're facing giants or fighting armies, and quite something else when you're watching people tear your world apart. God was chastening David, but David knew that God's power could help him in the hour of pain as well as in the hour of conquest. He wrote in one of his exile psalms, "Many are they who say of me, 'There is no help for him in God.'

But You, O Lord, are a shield for me, My glory and the
One who lifts up my head" (Ps. 3:2–3 NKJV).

—*Be Restored*, page 115

1. Why did David believe God hadn't forsaken him as God had Saul? How did David feel God's hand on his life in the midst of great trials and as he faced the wilderness ahead? How did his faith grow when he was forced to leave Jerusalem?

2. Choose one verse or phrase from 2 Samuel 15:1—16:14 that stands out to you. This could be something you're intrigued by, something that makes you uncomfortable, something that puzzles you, something that resonates with you, or just something you want to examine further. Write that here.

Going Deeper

From the Commentary

If ever a man was equipped to be a demagogue and lead people astray, that man was Absalom. He was a handsome man whose charm was difficult to resist (2 Sam. 14:25–26), and he had royal blood in his veins from both his father and his mother. The fact that he had no character wasn't important to most of the people who, like sheep, would follow anybody who told them what they wanted to hear and gave them what they wanted to have. Newspaper editor H. L. Mencken's definition of a demagogue is rather extreme, but he gets the point across: "One who preaches doctrines he knows to be untrue to men he knows to be idiots." Novelist James Fenimore Cooper expressed it accurately: "One who advances his own interests by affecting a deep devotion to the interests of the people."

Absalom was not only a consummate liar, but he was a patient man who was able to discern just the right hour to act. He waited two years before having Amnon murdered (13:23), and now he waited four years before openly rebelling against his father and seizing the throne (15:7). When you read the "exile psalms" of David, you get the impression that at this time King David was ill and didn't have his hands on the affairs of the kingdom, thus giving Absalom opportunity to move in and take over. With great skill, the egotistical prince used every device at his disposal to mesmerize the people and win their support.

—*Be Restored*, pages 115–16

3. Review 2 Samuel 15:1–12. How was Absalom's approach to gaining power similar to the way many people attempt to do this in modern times? What image did he craft for himself? In what ways was he merely a celebrity?

More to Consider: Since David wasn't available to the people, Absalom met them personally on the road to the city gate when they came early each morning to have their grievances examined and their cases tried. The city gate was the "city hall" of the ancient cities (Gen. 23:10; Deut. 22:15; 25:7; Ruth 4:1–12), and he knew he would encounter many disgruntled people there wondering why the court system wasn't functioning efficiently. Absalom would greet these visitors as old friends and find out where they came from and what their problems were. He agreed with all of them that their complaints were right and should be settled in their favor by the king's court. How was this an example of Absalom positioning himself for his future pursuit of the throne? In what ways is this similar to the manner in which some politicians act today? When people started to bow to him because he was the crown prince, he reached out his hand and stopped them, pulled them to himself, and kissed them (2 Sam. 15:5). How is this similar to the actions of Judas in the garden of Gethsemane? (See Matt. 26:47–50; Mark 14:45.)

From the Commentary

> It took only four years for Absalom's magnetism to draw together a large number of devoted followers throughout the whole land. The people Absalom met returned home and told their friends and neighbors that they had spoken personally to the crown prince, and over the four-year period, this kind of endorsement won Absalom many friends. His rapid success at influencing the minds and hearts of a nation warns us that one day a leader will arise who will control the minds of people around the world (Rev. 13:3; 2 Thess. 2). Even the people of Israel will be deceived and sign a covenant with this ruler, and then he will turn on them and seek to destroy them (Dan. 9:26–27).
>
> —*Be Restored*, page 117

4. How could Absalom have gained such a following so quickly? What is it about leaders that make them vulnerable to coups? How was the way people accepted Absalom an example of what Jesus later told the Jewish leaders of His day in John 5:43?

From Today's World

If Absalom were running for office today, his face would be plastered all over our media-saturated world. Politics is as much about celebrity as it is about substance, if not more so. This isn't just the case with national politics—it's even true in the local church, or perhaps in the workplace. Presenting a compelling image is what gets attention, and the substantive issues often play second fiddle to that image. Does presenting a good front work? Indeed it does, just as it did for Absalom, who likely made promises as grand as those you hear every election season in the United States today.

5. Why does image hold so much sway with the general populace? Is it a matter of laziness on the people's part—that they don't do their due diligence in vetting the candidates? Or is it because we've become an image-obsessed society? How does this play out in local and national politics? In the politics of the workplace? The local church? What are some steps we can take to make informed decisions about our leaders?

From the Commentary

Absalom's masterstroke was to win the support of Ahithophel, David's smartest counselor, and when the guests saw him at the feast, they felt confident that all was well. But Ahithophel did more than attend the celebration; he also joined Absalom in revolting against King David. It was probably Ahithophel who master-minded the entire operation. After all, David had violated Ahithophel's granddaughter Bathsheba and ordered her husband killed. (See 2 Sam. 23:34; 1 Chron. 3:5.) This was Ahithophel's great opportunity to avenge himself on David. However, in supporting Absalom, Ahithophel was rejecting Bathsheba's son Solomon, whom God would choose to be the next ruler of Israel. At the same time, Ahithophel was taking steps toward his own death, for like Judas, he rejected the true king and went out and committed suicide. (See 2 Sam. 17:23; Ps. 41:9; 55:12–14; Matt. 26:21–25; John 13:18; Acts 1:16.) Ahithophel had deceived David his king and sinned against the Lord, who had chosen David.

—*Be Restored*, page 118

6. What does this story tell us about the importance of choosing your friends and confidants wisely? How did Ahithophel take advantage of his relationship with David? Why did he shift his loyalty to Absalom? How is this similar to the way loyalties shift in modern politics? What should our process be when determining who deserves our loyalty? What role does seeking God's wisdom play into these decisions?

From the Commentary

> Absalom and Ahithophel had their trumpeters and mes-
> sengers ready to act, and at the signal, the word quickly
> spread throughout the land: "Absalom is king! He reigns
> from Hebron!" The anonymous messenger who informed
> David actually helped to save the king's life. However
> lethargic David may have been before now, he immedi-
> ately moved into action, because David always did his
> best during a crisis.
>
> —*Be Restored*, page 119

7. In what ways did David move into action after hearing about Absalom's
claim to the throne? How was this a wake-up call for David? What might
be a wake-up call for the church today?

From the Commentary

> David and the people with him escaped to the northeast,
> moving from Jerusalem opposite the direction of Hebron.
> When they came to the last house in the suburbs of

Jerusalem, they rested and David reviewed his troops. These included David's personal bodyguard (the Cherethites and the Pelethites, 2 Sam. 8:18; 23:22–23) as well as six hundred Philistines who had followed David from Gath and were under the command of Ittai (1 Sam. 27:2). Ittai assured David that they were completely loyal to the king. This Gentile's testimony of fidelity to David (2 Sam. 15:21) is one of the great confessions of faith and faithfulness found in Scripture and ranks with that of Ruth (Ruth 1:16) and the Roman centurion (Matt. 8:5–13).

—*Be Restored*, page 120

8. David's story is fraught with danger. What did God teach him through these challenging seasons and crises? What do we learn about ourselves when we're in danger? What do we learn about God?

More to Consider: The key phrase in 2 Samuel 15:13–23 is "marched on" or "crossed." Variations of these terms are used nine times in 2 Samuel 15. David and his people crossed the Kidron (v. 23), which in winter flowed powerfully on the east side of Jerusalem and had to be crossed to reach the Mount of Olives. How does this scene remind us of Jesus' experience when He went to the garden (John 18:1)? David's own son had betrayed him along with his friend and confidential adviser, and the foolish people, for whom the king had done so much, were ignorant of what was going on. How is this circumstance another example of David's life showing similarities to Christ's? (See Luke 23:34.)

From the Commentary

When you read David's exile psalms, you can't help but see his trust in God and his conviction that, no matter how disordered and disturbed everything was, the Lord was still on His throne. No matter how David felt, he knew that the Lord would always keep His covenant and fulfill His promises. Psalm 4 might well have been the song David sang to God that first evening away from home, and Psalm 3 what he prayed the next morning. In Psalms 41 and 55, he poured out his heart to the Lord, and the Lord heard him and answered in His time. Psalms 61, 62, and 63 allow us to look into David's troubled heart as he asks God for guidance and strength. Note that each of these three psalms ends with a strong affirmation of faith in the Lord. Today we can have courage and assurance in our own times of difficulty as we see how the Lord responded to David and his great needs.

—*Be Restored*, page 121

9. Review 2 Samuel 15:24—16:14. What do we learn about God's faithfulness through David's exile story? How did David deal with this second exile? What are some of the "exiles" that we as believers face today? What can we learn from David's story to help us through those times? (See the psalms noted in the previous commentary excerpt.)

From the Commentary

David was rejected by his own people and betrayed by his own familiar friend. He gave up everything for the sake of the people and would have surrendered his own life to save his rebellious son who deserved to die. Like Jesus, David crossed the Kidron and went up Mount Olivet. He was falsely accused and shamefully treated, and yet he submitted to the sovereign will of God. "Who, when He was reviled, did not revile in return; when He suffered, He did not threaten, but committed Himself to Him who judges righteously" (1 Peter 2:23 NKJV).

David had lost his throne, but Jehovah God was still on the throne and would keep His promises with His servant. Faithful to His covenant, the Lord remembered David and all the hardships that he endured (Ps. 132:1), and He remembers us today.

—*Be Restored*, page 127

10. Summarize the suffering that David endured in his life so far. What did all this suffering accomplish? In what ways was David's life similar to Jesus'? In what ways was it dramatically different? What can we learn about how to live in faith from David's story? What can we learn about God's sovereignty? His forgiveness?

Looking Inward

Take a moment to reflect on all that you've explored thus far in this study of 2 Samuel 15:1—16:14. Review your notes and answers and think about how each of these things matters in your life today.

Tips for Small Groups: To get the most out of this section, form pairs or trios and have group members take turns answering these questions. Be honest and as open as you can in this discussion, but most of all, be encouraging and supportive of others. Be sensitive to those who are going through particularly difficult times and don't press for people to speak if they're uncomfortable doing so.

11. Do you ever focus more on image than substance? Explain. What is it about your own image that matters most to you? How do you "cultivate"

an image? How do you cultivate character? How does your relationship with God determine the approach you choose?

12. Think about a time when someone you trusted betrayed that trust. How did that make you feel? Had you missed any signs about their lack of loyalty? If so, what might you have done differently? What role does grace play in such situations? What role does caution play? How can God's Word help you make wise decisions about whom you trust?

13. David spent two long seasons of his life in exile. Have you ever felt as if you were in exile? Describe the situation. Where was God during that time? How did you seek Him when you felt alone or betrayed or lost? What lessons did you learn through your exile?

Going Forward

14. Think of one or two things that you have learned that you'd like to work on in the coming week. Remember that this is all about quality, not quantity. It's better to work on one specific area of life and do it well than to work on many and do poorly (or to be so overwhelmed that you simply don't try).

Do you want to focus on substance rather than image? Be specific. Go back through 2 Samuel 15:1—16:14 and put a star next to the phrase or verse that is most encouraging to you. Consider memorizing this verse.

Real-Life Application Ideas: During this week, pay special attention to the divide between image and substance. This isn't a time to cast judgment on others, but a time to observe quietly how people present themselves in the workplace, in the church, or in the public eye. Use the time to ask God for wisdom in determining what really matters and how to pursue the truth rather than pursue a favorable image. This is harder than it sounds, and it would be good to invite a close friend or family member into this exercise so you don't fall into the trap of pointing fingers at others. God is a God of substance, not image. Start there.

Seeking Help

15. Write a prayer below (or simply pray one in silence), inviting God to work on your mind and heart in those areas you've noted in the Going Forward section. Be honest about your desires and fears.

Notes for Small Groups:

- *Look for ways to put into practice the things you wrote in the Going Forward section. Talk with other group members about your ideas and commit to being accountable to one another.*

- *During the coming week, ask the Holy Spirit to continue to reveal truth to you from what you've read and studied.*

- *Before you start the next lesson, read 2 Samuel 16:15—19:40. For more in-depth lesson preparation, read chapters 8 and 9, "David's Bittersweet Victory" and "David's Return and Renewed Problems," in* Be Restored.

Return
(2 SAMUEL 16:15—19:40)

Before you begin ...
- *Pray for the Holy Spirit to reveal truth and wisdom as you go through this lesson.*
- *Read 2 Samuel 16:15—19:40. This lesson references chapters 8 and 9 in* Be Restored. *It will be helpful for you to have your Bible and a copy of the commentary available as you work through this lesson.*

Getting Started

From the Commentary

David's army and Absalom's army were about to engage in battle in a civil war that neither father nor son could win, but both sides could lose. If David won, it meant death for his son Absalom and his friend Ahithophel; if Absalom won, it could mean death for David and other members of his family.

Absalom was trusting his charm, his popularity, his army,

and the wisdom of Ahithophel, but David was trusting the Lord. "Hear my cry, O God; attend to my prayer. From the end of the earth I will cry to You, when my heart is overwhelmed; lead me to the rock that is higher than I" (Ps. 61:1–2 NKJV).

—*Be Restored*, pages 131–32

1. Why might it have been tempting for Absalom to trust his charm and popularity to lead him to victory? How is this similar to the way people often enter conflict today? What does it look like for us to actively trust God in the midst of our battles?

2. Choose one verse or phrase from 2 Samuel 16:15—19:40 that stands out to you. This could be something you're intrigued by, something that makes you uncomfortable, something that puzzles you, something that resonates with you, or just something you want to examine further. Write that here.

Going Deeper

From the Commentary

> Absalom had two important tasks to perform before he could rule the kingdom of Israel. The first was that he had to seize his father's throne and let it be known that he was officially the king. Unlike his father David, who sought the mind of the Lord through the Urim and Thummim or from a prophet, Absalom looked to human experience and wisdom—and from a human point of view, Ahithophel was among the very best. However, Ahithophel didn't seek the mind of the Lord, nor did he want the will of the Lord. His primary goal was to avenge himself against David for the sin he had committed against his granddaughter Bathsheba and her husband, Uriah the Hittite.
>
> —*Be Restored*, page 133

3. Why was Absalom drawn to following human wisdom and experience? What mistakes did that lead Absalom to make in 2 Samuel 16:15—17:14? How can a desire for revenge cloud a person's vision? What does this story teach us about the risks of trusting people who don't care about God?

More to Consider: It was customary for a new king to inherit the previous king's wives and harem, so when Absalom followed Ahithophel's counsel, he was declaring that he was now king of Israel. (See 2 Sam. 3:7; 12:8.) What message was Absalom giving to his father through this act? What was Absalom telling his followers?

From the Commentary

Humanly speaking, if Absalom had followed Ahithophel's plan, David would have been slain and Absalom's problems solved. But David had prayed that God would turn Ahithophel's counsel into foolishness (2 Sam. 15:31), and God used Hushai to do just that. Note that Ahithophel put himself front and center by using phrases like "Let me now choose … I will arise … I will come …" and so on. He wanted to be the general of the army because he wanted personally to supervise the murder of his enemy King David. His plan was a good one: use a small army that could move swiftly, attack suddenly at night, and have David's death as the one great goal. Ahithophel would then bring back David's followers, and they would swear loyalty to the new king. It would be a quick victory, and very little blood would be shed.

Hushai wasn't in the room when Ahithophel outlined his plan, so Absalom called him in and told him what his favorite counselor had said.

—*Be Restored*, page 134

4. How did God direct Hushai in 2 Samuel 17:7–13? Why was Absalom so easily led away from Ahithophel's plan, despite how neatly it would have worked for him? What role did Absalom's ego play in how the story unfolded?

From the Commentary

David and his people were camped at the fords of the Jordan, about twenty miles from Jerusalem, and the two runners were waiting at En Rogel in the Kidron Valley, less than a mile from Jerusalem. Hushai gave the message to the two priests and told them to tell David to cross over the Jordan as quickly as possible. He was not to delay. If Absalom changed his mind and adopted Ahithophel's plan, then all might be lost. Zadok and Abiathar told an anonymous maidservant; she took the message to Jonathan and Ahimaaz, who immediately ran a mile south to the house of a collaborator in Bahurim. However, a young man saw them leave and recognized the priests' sons. Wanting to impress the new king, he told Absalom what was happening, and Absalom's guards started out after the two young men.

At this point, the account reads like the story of the two spies recorded in Joshua 2. Rahab hid the two spies under stalks of flax on the roof of her house. The wife in Bahurim hid the two runners in a cistern, covered the opening with a cloth, and sprinkled grain on the cloth. The cloth looked like it was there to provide a place to dry grain in the sun. Not obligated to assist Absalom in his evil plans, the woman sent the guards off in the wrong direction, and the young men were saved. They arrived at David's camp, gave the king the facts, and urged him to cross the Jordan immediately, which he did. The guards returned to Jerusalem empty-handed, but Absalom didn't see their failure as a serious problem.

—*Be Restored*, page 136

5. What does this sequence of events teach us about God's timing? About how He uses people in creative ways to accomplish His will? Why didn't Absalom see the guards' empty-handed return as a problem? Why was that a mistake on his part?

From the Commentary

Knowing that the enemy was soon to arrive, David numbered his troops, divided them into three companies, and placed Joab, Abishai, and Ittai as their commanders. Whatever approach Absalom and Amasa used, David's men would be able to maneuver and help each other. David offered to accompany the army, but the people told him to stay in a place of safety in the walled city. (See 2 Sam. 21:15–17, which occurred long before Absalom's rebellion.) "There are ten thousand of us but only one of you!" they argued. They knew that Absalom's soldiers would go after the king and not worry about the soldiers. If David stayed in the city, he could send out reinforcements if they were needed. David accepted their decisions; he didn't want to fight his son anyway.

But neither did he want the army to fight his son. Absalom had stood at the gate in Jerusalem and attacked his father (2 Sam. 15:1–6); now David stood at a city gate and instructed the soldiers to go easy on Absalom. Absalom certainly hadn't been gentle with his father! He had murdered Amnon, driven David out of Jerusalem, seized his throne, violated David's concubines, and now he was out to kill David.

—*Be Restored*, page 138

6. In what ways was David's request that the soldiers "go easy" on Absalom evidence that he was a man after God's heart? How was it an example of

grace? (See Ps. 103:1–14.) In what ways did it reveal David's weakness as a father who pampered his sons?

From the Commentary

The text says that David trembled violently when he comprehended that Absalom had been slain. No doubt he had prayed that the worst would not happen, but it happened just the same. In one sense, David pronounced his own sentence when he said to Nathan, "And he shall restore the lamb fourfold" (2 Sam. 12:6), for this was the final payment of David's great debt. The baby had died, Tamar was raped, Amnon was slain, and now Absalom was dead. David tasted once again the pain of forgiven sin.

David's tears reveal the broken heart of a loving father. Speaking about David's sorrow, Charles Spurgeon said, "It would be wiser to sympathize, as far as we can, than to sit in judgment upon a case which has never been our own." David wept when he heard about the death of Jonathan and Saul (2 Sam. 1:11–12), the murder of Abner (3:32), and the murder of Amnon (13:33–36), so why shouldn't he weep over the death of his beloved son Absalom? Once again, we see the heart of God revealed in the heart of David, for Christ died for us when we were sinners and living as the enemies of God (Rom. 5:7–10). David would have died for Absalom, but Jesus *did die for us!*

—*Be Restored*, pages 142

7. Was David's response to his son's death excessive? Why wouldn't he permit himself to be comforted? What did this reveal about David's character? About his remorse for the decisions he'd made years before?

From the Commentary

When David finally arrived in Jerusalem, it was a signal to the nation that the rebellion was ended and their true king was back on the throne. But en route to Jerusalem, David made some royal decisions that sent out other important messages to the people. His first message was that he wanted his kingdom to be a united people. The old prejudices and animosities must be buried and the nation must be united behind its king. Within the tribes, the people were divided between the followers of Absalom and the followers of David (2 Sam. 19:9–10), and the old division between the ten tribes (Israel) and Judah still persisted (vv. 40–43).

—*Be Restored*, page 147

8. Review 2 Samuel 19:9–15. Why was unity such an important theme of David's return to the throne? How is the divided loyalty David faced similar to what often transpires in our churches today? How can today's church pursue unity?

From the Commentary

The news of this appointment must have shocked the leaders of the nation and then brought them great relief, for it meant that David was pardoning all the officials who had followed Absalom. Amasa had been Absalom's general whose assignment it had been to search for David and destroy him, but now David was making his nephew (and Joab's cousin) the leader of his great army.

—*Be Restored*, page 148

9. What message did David give when he pardoned those who had followed Absalom? But why did he choose to replace Joab? How did David know who was and wasn't trustworthy? What does this tell us about David's relationship with God at this point in his life?

From the Commentary

Not only were the men of Judah at the Jordan to welcome David, but his enemy Shimei the Benjamite was there with a thousand men from his tribe (see 2 Sam. 16:5–14). Ziba, the land manager for Mephibosheth (9:1–10), was also in the crowd with his fifteen sons and twenty servants, and they crossed the river to meet him on the western shore and help escort him to the other side. Somebody provided a ferryboat that went back and forth across the Jordan to carry the king's household so they wouldn't have to ford the river. When David arrived on the western bank of the river, Shimei prostrated himself and begged for mercy.

There's no doubt that Shimei deserved to be killed for the way he treated David (Ex. 22:28), and Abishai was willing to do the job, but David stopped his nephew just as he had done before (2 Sam. 16:9). The first time David stopped Abishai, his reason was that the Lord had told Shimei to curse the king, so David would take his abuse as from the hand of the Lord. But now his reason for sparing Shimei was because it was a day of rejoicing, not a day of revenge. But even more, by pardoning Shimei, King David was offering a general amnesty to all who had supported Absalom during the rebellion.

—*Be Restored*, pages 149–50

10. Review 2 Samuel 19:16–23. How did David demonstrate godly forgiveness in his actions? Did the various people deserve amnesty? Why or why not? In what ways was this another example of David's symbolic representation of the coming Christ?

Looking Inward

Take a moment to reflect on all that you've explored thus far in this study of 2 Samuel 16:15—19:40. Review your notes and answers and think about how each of these things matters in your life today.

Tips for Small Groups: To get the most out of this section, form pairs or trios and have group members take turns answering these questions. Be honest and as open as you can in this discussion, but most of all, be encouraging and supportive of others. Be sensitive to those who are going through particularly difficult times and don't press for people to speak if they're uncomfortable doing so.

11. Have you ever been charmed by someone who was later revealed to have an agenda you didn't agree with? How was that situation resolved? What is it about a person's charm that can blind you to the truth? How is this similar to the way Satan acted in the garden of Eden?

12. Throughout the Bible, we see examples of God using people who aren't followers to help move His narrative forward. Have you ever been guided or directed toward God by someone who wasn't a believer? Describe that situation. What did this teach you about God's will? About how to hear God's voice in a world that's often seemingly godless?

13. David forgave people who previously aligned themselves with his traitorous son. Is there anyone you should forgive, giving the relationship a fresh start or just deciding not to get back at that person? How is that exactly like what God has done for you with Jesus' death and resurrection?

Going Forward

14. Think of one or two things that you have learned that you'd like to work on in the coming week. Remember that this is all about quality, not quantity. It's better to work on one specific area of life and do it well than to work on many and do poorly (or to be so overwhelmed that you simply don't try).

Do you want to forgive those who have hurt you in the past? Be specific. Go back through 2 Samuel 16:15—19:40 and put a star next to the phrase or verse that is most encouraging to you. Consider memorizing this verse.

Real-Life Application Ideas: This week, ask God to help you know who in your life deserves amnesty or forgiveness. Perhaps someone wronged you at work, or maybe a family member hurt you with his or her words. Be intentional with your forgiveness. In some cases this might mean actually offering forgiveness to someone one to one. But in most cases, it's just a matter of silently forgiving the person and wiping the slate clean so you can reestablish a healthy relationship. The key is to be intentional as you offer grace.

Seeking Help

15. Write a prayer below (or simply pray one in silence), inviting God to work on your mind and heart in those areas you've noted in the Going Forward section. Be honest about your desires and fears.

Notes for Small Groups:

- *Look for ways to put into practice the things you wrote in the Going Forward section. Talk with other group members about your ideas and commit to being accountable to one another.*

- *During the coming week, ask the Holy Spirit to continue to reveal truth to you from what you've read and studied.*

- *Before you start the next lesson, read 2 Samuel 19:41—22:51 and 1 Chronicles 20:4–8. (Also read Psalm 18 for more context.) For more in-depth lesson preparation, read chapters 10 and 11, "David's New Struggles" and "David's Song of Victory," in* Be Restored.

Victory

(2 SAMUEL 19:41—22:51; 1 CHRONICLES 20:4–8)

Before you begin ...
- *Pray for the Holy Spirit to reveal truth and wisdom as you go through this lesson.*
- *Read 2 Samuel 19:41—22:51 and 1 Chronicles 20:4–8. (Also read Psalm 18 for more context.) This lesson references chapters 10 and 11 in* Be Restored. *It will be helpful for you to have your Bible and a copy of the commentary available as you work through this lesson.*

Getting Started

From the Commentary

A crisis will bring out the best in some people and the worst in others. The representatives of the tribes were gathered at Gilgal to escort their king back to Jerusalem, and instead of rejoicing at the victory God had given His people, the tribes were fighting among themselves. The "men of Israel" were the ten northern tribes, and they were angry at the southern tribe of Judah, which had also absorbed the tribe of Simeon. Israel was angry because Judah had not waited for them to arrive on the scene to help take David home. Judah had "kidnapped" the king and had ignored and insulted the other ten tribes. Judah replied that David was from their tribe, so they had the greater responsibility to care for him. Israel argued that they had ten shares in David but Judah had only two, as though the king were some kind of security on the stock market. Apparently nobody urged the tribes to call on Jehovah for His help and to remember that Gilgal was the place where Israel had made a new beginning in Joshua's day (Josh. 3—5).

—*Be Restored*, pages 157–58

1. Review 2 Samuel 19:41—20:3, 14–26. Why is it that people (in this case, tribes of people) are so quick to fight among themselves over trivial issues? What causes men and women to want to be "right" above all else? Why didn't the tribes in David's time seek God's counsel first? How do we know when we're seeking God's will rather than simply wanting to prove we're "right"?

More to Consider: The conflict between Judah and Israel had deep roots, just like the political conflicts that divide many nations today. When King Saul assembled his first army, it was divided between Israel and Judah (1 Sam. 11:8), and this division continued throughout his reign (15:4; 17:52). After the death of Saul, the ten tribes of Israel followed Saul's son Ish-Bosheth, while Judah followed David (2 Sam. 2:10–11). How does what Jesus said in Matthew 12:25 apply to the situation in David's time? How does it apply to us today? What are the church's "divided kingdoms"?

2. Choose one verse or phrase from 2 Samuel 19:41—22:51; 1 Chronicles 20:4–8; or Psalm 18 that stands out to you. This could be something you're intrigued by, something that makes you uncomfortable, something that puzzles you, something that resonates with you, or just something you want to examine further. Write that here.

Going Deeper

From the Commentary

Second Samuel closes with a record of two national calamities—a drought caused by King Saul's sin (21:1–14) and a plague caused by King David's sin (24:1–25).

Between these two tragic events, the writer gives us a summary of four victories (21:15–22) and a list of David's mighty men (23:8–39), as well as two psalms written by David (22:1—23:7). Once again we see David the soldier, the singer, and the sinner.

Nowhere in Scripture are we told when or why Saul slaughtered the Gibeonites and thus broke the vow that Israel had made with them in Joshua's day (Josh. 9). Joshua tried to make the best of his mistake, because he put the Gibeonites to work as woodcutters and water carriers, but Israel's vow obligated them before God to protect the Gibeonites (Josh. 10). Saul killed several Gibeonites but intended to wipe them all out, so it was a case of ethnic cleansing and genocide.

Saul's religious life is a puzzle. Attempting to appear very godly, he would make foolish vows that nobody should keep (1 Sam. 14:24–35), while at the same time he didn't obey the clear commands of the Lord (1 Sam. 13; 15). He was commanded to slay the Amalekites and didn't, yet he tried to exterminate the Gibeonites.

—*Be Restored*, pages 161–62

3. Why does the Bible record the result of Saul's and David's sins here? What is the message to God's people in highlighting these events? What do we learn about both David and Saul from these stories? How were their lives similar? In what ways were they different?

From the Commentary

The four conflicts in 2 Samuel 21:15–22 and 1 Chronicles 20:4–8 took place much earlier in David's reign, probably after he made Jerusalem his capital and the Philistines opposed his rise to power. All four involve descendants of the giants from Philistia, one of whom was a brother of Goliath (2 Sam. 21:19).

In the first conflict (2 Sam. 21:15–17), David fought so much that he grew faint, because the Philistines would focus on him rather than the other soldiers. Ishbi-benob wanted to slay David and had a bronze spear that weighed seven and a half pounds. However David's nephew Abishai, who more than once irritated David, came to the king's rescue and killed the giant. It was then that the military leaders decided the king was too vulnerable and valuable to be sacrificed on the battlefield. The king was the "lamp of Israel" and had to be protected. (See 1 Kings 11:36; 15:4; 2 Kings 8:19; 2 Chron. 21:7.)

The second contest with the Philistines (2 Sam. 21:18; 1 Chron. 20:4) took place at Gob, a site we can't locate with any accuracy, where Israel won the battle because one of David's mighty men killed the giant. (See 1 Chron. 11:29.) The fact that the names of these giants were preserved shows that they were well-known warriors.

The third conflict with the Philistines (2 Sam. 21:19) was again at Gob, and this time the brother of Goliath (1 Chron. 20:5) is the giant that was slain. We know little about Elhanan except that he came from Bethlehem and was one of David's mighty men (2 Sam. 23:24).

The fourth battle took place in Gath in enemy territory (2 Sam. 21:20–22; 1 Chron. 20:6–8), and David's nephew Jonathan killed the giant who had, like Goliath, defied Israel and Israel's God. (See 1 Sam. 17:10.)

—*Be Restored*, pages 164–65

4. Why was it wise for David to stop fighting alongside his men on the battlefield? How did retiring from the battlefield affect David? (See 2 Sam. 11.) Why was it good to let other men achieve heroic victories against giants? How might David have had mixed feelings about those heroic victories?

From the Commentary

First Samuel 2 records the song Hannah sang when she brought her son Samuel to serve the Lord at the tabernacle, and 2 Samuel 22 records the song of David after the Lord helped him defeat his enemies (v. 1; Ps. 18).

—*Be Restored*, page 169

5. What is the significance of including these songs of praise in books full of burdens and bloodshed? What does this teach us about the role of praise? About the presence of God before, during, and after our battles?

From the Commentary

"Deliver" is a key word in David's song (2 Sam. 22:1, 2, 18, 20, 44, 49), and it carries with it the meanings of "drawing out of danger, snatching, taking away, allowing to escape." For at least ten years before he became king, David was pursued by Saul and his army, and the record shows that Saul tried to kill David at least five times. (See 1 Sam. 18:10–11; 19:8–24.) After he became king, David had to wage war against the Philistines, the Ammonites, the Syrians, the Moabites, and the Edomites, and God enabled him to triumph over all his enemies.

—*Be Restored*, page 170

6. Review 2 Samuel 22:1–19. How did David praise the Lord in this passage? What pictures did he paint of his relationship with God? Why would this have been significant to the Israelites during this time in their history? How is it significant for us today?

More to Consider: Read Genesis 49:24 and Deuteronomy 32:4, 15, 18, 30–31. Why is the imagery of "rock" used so often in Scripture? What does this image tell us about our hope? About our trust in God? About God Himself?

From the Commentary

What do you do when you're drowning in a flood of opposition? *You call on the Lord and trust Him for the help you need* (2 Sam. 22:7). David was a man of prayer who depended on the Lord for wisdom, strength, and deliverance, and the Lord never failed him. Why did God wait all those years before delivering David and putting him on the throne? For one thing, the Lord was building himself a leader, and this could be done only by means of trial, suffering, and battle. But the Lord also had His own timetable, for "when the fullness of the time had come" (Gal. 4:4 NKJV), out of David's family the Messiah would come to the world.

When the Lord answered David's cries and delivered him from Saul and the enemies of the people of God, it was like a great thunderstorm being released over the land (2 Sam. 22:8–20).

—*Be Restored*, page 171

7. How did David describe God's intervention in 2 Samuel 22:8–9? What was God's demeanor during this intervention? (See also Ps. 74:1; 140:10.)

What did this reveal about God's character? About how David viewed God during this time?

From the Commentary

> For at least ten years, David had been in tight places, but now the Lord had brought him out "into a spacious place" (2 Sam. 22:20 NIV). God could give him a larger place because David had been enlarged in his own life through his experiences of trial and testing. "Thou hast enlarged me when I was in distress" (Ps. 4:1). David had often cried out, "The troubles of my heart are enlarged," but at the same time, God was enlarging His servant and preparing him for a bigger place (Ps. 18:19, 36). "I called on the Lord in distress; the Lord answered me and set me in a broad place" (Ps. 118:5 NKJV). In the school of life, God promotes those who, in times of difficulty, learn the lessons of faith and patience (Heb. 6:12), and David had learned his lessons well.
>
> —*Be Restored*, page 172

8. Read 2 Samuel 22:21–25. Was David bragging in this passage? Why or why not? In what ways was David being thankful here? How had David sought to please the Lord, obey His law, and trust His promises in the past? How do these verses describe David as a man of integrity (see Ps. 78:72), a man after God's own heart (1 Sam. 13:14)?

From the Commentary

> The Lord never violates His own attributes. God deals with people according to their attitudes and their actions. David was merciful to Saul and spared his life on at least two occasions, and the Lord was merciful to David. "Blessed are the merciful: for they shall obtain mercy" (Matt. 5:7). David was faithful to the Lord, and the Lord was faithful to him. David was upright; he was single-hearted when it came to serving God. He was not sinless—no man or woman on earth is—but he was blameless in his motives and loyal to the Lord. In that sense, his heart was pure: "Blessed are the pure in heart: for they shall see God" (Matt. 5:8).
>
> —*Be Restored*, page 173

9. Review 2 Samuel 22:26–28. What do we learn about the word "blameless" from the fact that David could call himself blameless? In what ways was he blameless? How does 2 Samuel show David's humility? How did David's submission to God affect his life journey?

From the Commentary

> It is one thing to fight wars and defeat the enemy, but it is quite something else to keep these nations under control. David not only had to unify and lead the twelve tribes of Israel, but he also had to deal with the nations that were subjected to Israel.

> The Gentile nations didn't want a king on the throne of Israel, especially a brilliant strategist, brave warrior, and beloved leader like David. However, God not only established him on the throne, but also promised him a dynasty that would never end. The Lord promised David a throne, and He kept His promise. He also helped David to unite his own people and deal with those who were still loyal to Saul. The word "strangers" in 2 Samuel 22:45–46 means "foreigners" and refers to Gentile nations. The Lord's victories frightened these peoples and drove them

into hiding places. Eventually they would come out of their feeble fortresses and submit to David.

David's shout of praise, "The Lord lives" (v. 47 NKJV), was his bold witness to these subjected peoples that their dead idols could not save them or protect them (see Ps. 115). Only Jehovah, the God of Israel, is the true and living God, and David's victories and enthronement proved that God was with him. David was always careful not to exalt himself, but to exalt the Lord. David closed his song with high and holy praise for the Lord God of Israel. He exalted the Lord, and the Lord exalted him (Matt. 6:33; 1 Sam. 2:30). If we magnify our own name or our own deeds, we will sin; but if the Lord magnifies us, we can bring glory to His name (Josh. 3:7).

God's sovereign choice of David to be king, and His dynastic covenant with him, form the foundation for all that God did for His servant. Israel was called to be a witness to the nations, and it was David's responsibility to build a kingdom that would honor the name of the Lord. It's too bad that because of his sin with Bathsheba he brought reproach to God's name (2 Sam. 12:14). Nevertheless, David was God's king and God's anointed, and the covenant between God and David still stands and will ultimately be fulfilled in the reign of Jesus Christ in His kingdom.

—*Be Restored*, pages 176–77

10. Review 2 Samuel 22:44–51. How does this passage reveal how God established David as a leader? What does it mean to be "established" by God? How does God establish leaders today?

Looking Inward

Take a moment to reflect on all that you've explored thus far in this study of 2 Samuel 19:41—22:51; 1 Chronicles 20:4–8; and Psalm 18. Review your notes and answers and think about how each of these things matters in your life today.

> *Tips for Small Groups: To get the most out of this section, form pairs or trios and have group members take turns answering these questions. Be honest and as open as you can in this discussion, but most of all, be encouraging and supportive of others. Be sensitive to those who are going through particularly difficult times and don't press for people to speak if they're uncomfortable doing so.*

11. Describe a time when you were among a group of people squabbling over trivial issues. What caused the disagreement? How was it resolved? Have you experienced this in your church? How can you tell when a group is actually making progress in a discussion and when it's simply mired in

disagreement? How can God's Word direct groups who just refuse to agree with one another?

12. Is it easy for you to praise God when you've been enduring hardship? Why or why not? Why is it important to praise God when things are looking bleak or when you're being stretched or tested? How have you experienced God's nearness in these times?

13. What does it take to be blameless? Can you legitimately call yourself blameless, though not sinless? Why or why not? How can you pursue a life of righteousness and humility?

Going Forward

14. Think of one or two things that you have learned that you'd like to work on in the coming week. Remember that this is all about quality, not quantity. It's better to work on one specific area of life and do it well than to work on many and do poorly (or to be so overwhelmed that you simply don't try).

Do you want to know if you're meant to be a leader? Be specific. Go back through 2 Samuel 19:41—22:51; 1 Chronicles 20:4–8; and Psalm 18 and put a star next to the phrase or verse that is most encouraging to you. Consider memorizing this verse.

Real-Life Application Ideas: Church leaders face lots of challenges, from simple disagreement to outright rebellion. But godly leaders keep pressing forward, trusting God's guidance as they attempt to do His will. This week, celebrate the leaders in your life, thanking them for their roles in shaping your faith and asking God to protect them and bless them for all they do in His name. Then make it a habit to honor your leaders whenever possible.

Seeking Help

15. Write a prayer below (or simply pray one in silence), inviting God to work on your mind and heart in those areas you've noted in the Going Forward section. Be honest about your desires and fears.

> *Notes for Small Groups:*
> * *Look for ways to put into practice the things you wrote in the Going Forward section. Talk with other group members about your ideas and commit to being accountable to one another.*
> * *During the coming week, ask the Holy Spirit to continue to reveal truth to you from what you've read and studied.*
> * *Before you start the next lesson, read 2 Samuel 23—24 and 1 Chronicles 11:10–41; 21—29. For more in-depth lesson preparation, read chapters 12 and 13, "David's Memories and Mistakes" and "David's Legacy," in* Be Restored.

Legacy
(2 SAMUEL 23—24; 1 CHRONICLES 11:10–41; 21—29)

Before you begin …

- *Pray for the Holy Spirit to reveal truth and wisdom as you go through this lesson.*
- *Read 2 Samuel 23—24 and 1 Chronicles 11:10–41; 21—29. This lesson references chapters 12 and 13 in* Be Restored. *It will be helpful for you to have your Bible and a copy of the commentary available as you work through this lesson.*

Getting Started

From the Commentary

At least seventy-three of the psalms in the book of Psalms are assigned to David, but his last one is found only here in 2 Samuel 23. The phrase "the last words of David" means "his last inspired written words from the Lord." The psalm may have been written during the closing days of his life, shortly before he died. Since the theme of the psalm is godly leadership, he may have written it especially for Solomon, but it has much to say to all of God's people today.

David never ceased to marvel that God would call him to become the king of Israel, to lead God's people, fight God's battles, and even help to write God's Word. It was through David's descendants that God brought the Messiah into the world. From the human point of view, David was a nobody, a shepherd, the youngest of eight sons in an ordinary Jewish family; nevertheless, God selected him and made him to become Israel's greatest king. The Lord had given David skillful hands and a heart of integrity (Ps. 78:70–72) and equipped him to know and do His will. As the son of Jesse, David was a member of the royal tribe of Judah, something that was not true of his predecessor Saul. (See Gen. 49:10.)

—*Be Restored*, pages 181–82

1. Review 2 Samuel 23:1–7. What does this song tell us about David? What was important to him at the end of his life? How had he experienced what the song says?

More to Consider: Dr. A. W. Tozer said, "Never follow any leader until you see the oil on his forehead." How does this quote apply to David's role as leader? Read 1 John 2:17. What does this verse teach us about godly leadership? How are leaders "trained by the Lord"?

2. Choose one verse or phrase from 2 Samuel 23—24 or 1 Chronicles 11:10–41; 21—29 that stands out to you. This could be something you're intrigued by, something that makes you uncomfortable, something that puzzles you, something that resonates with you, or just something you want to examine further. Write that here.

Going Deeper

From the Commentary

God didn't train David just to put him on display, but because He had important work for him to do; and so it is with every true leader. David was to rule over God's own people, "the sheep of his pasture" (Ps. 100:3), which is an awesome responsibility. It demands character and integrity ("just" = righteous) and a submissive attitude toward the Lord ("the fear of God"; 2 Sam. 23:3). Without righteousness and the fear of God, a leader becomes a dictator and abuses God's people, driving them like cattle instead of leading them like sheep. David was a ruler who served and a servant who ruled, and he had the welfare of his people on his heart (2 Sam. 24:17). It encourages me today to see that even secular business specialists are comparing effective leaders to shepherds who care.

—*Be Restored*, pages 183–84

3. What metaphor did David use to picture the work of the leader in 2 Samuel 23:4–7? How did David exemplify this principle in his life? How might this also remind us of what happened when Jesus came to earth? (See Ps. 72:5–7; Isa. 9:2; 58:8; 60:1, 19; Mal. 4:1–3; Matt. 4:13–16; Luke 2:29–32.)

From the Commentary

Second Samuel 23:8–39 and 1 Chronicles 11:10–47 list the names and some of the exploits of the leading men who followed David and stood with him during the difficult years of exile and during his reign. Here's a brief look at three of those men:

Josheb-Basshebeth (NKJV) is named first; he was also known as Adino and Jashobeam (2 Sam. 23:8; 1 Chron. 11:11). He was chief of the captains in David's army and was famous for killing eight hundred enemy soldiers "at one time." First Chronicles 11:11 says he killed three hundred men. As we've already noted, the transmission of numbers from manuscript to manuscript by copyists sometimes led to these minor differences. Did the fear of the Lord drive all these men over a cliff, or did Jashobeam's courage inspire others to enter the battle, and he got the credit for the victory? How he accomplished this feat isn't disclosed, but it's unlikely that he killed them one at a time with his spear.

Eleazar (2 Sam. 23:9–10) was from the tribe of Benjamin and fought beside David against the Philistines, probably at Pas Dammim (1 Sam. 17:1; 1 Chron. 11:12–13). While many of the Israelite soldiers were retreating, he remained in his place and fought until the sword was "welded" to his hand. The Lord honored the faith and courage of David and Eleazar and gave Israel a great victory, after which the other soldiers returned to the field to strip the dead and claim the spoils. Like David, Eleazar wasn't selfish about sharing the spoils of battle, because the victory had come from the Lord (1 Sam. 30:21–25).

The third mighty man was Shammah (2 Sam. 23:11–12), who also was used of the Lord to bring victory at Pas Dammim (1 Chron. 11:13–14). But why risk your life to defend a field of lentils and barley? Because the land belonged to the Lord (Lev. 25:23) and was given to Israel to use for His glory (Lev. 18:24–30). Shammah didn't want the Philistines to control what belonged to Jehovah, for the Jews were stewards of God's land. To respect the land meant to honor the Lord and His covenant with Israel.

—*Be Restored*, pages 185–86

4. What can we learn about David's leadership from these stories of his men? What can you learn about the leaders in your church based on the people whom they have mentored or taught? What kind of legacy does a great leader leave behind?

From the Commentary

Second Samuel 24:1 states that God incited David to number the people, while 1 Chronicles 21:1 names Satan as the culprit. Both are true: God permitted Satan to tempt David in order to accomplish the purposes He had in mind. Satan certainly opposed God's people throughout all of Old Testament history, but this is one of four instances in the Old Testament where Satan is named specifically and seen openly at work.

—*Be Restored*, page 191

5. Why would God allow Satan to tempt David in order to accomplish His will? Why not choose a different method to direct David's path? How is this similar to the stories of Eve (Gen. 3), Job (Job 1—2), and Joshua the high priest (Zech. 3)?

From the Commentary

Some Bible readers today might be tempted to scan 1 Chronicles 22—29, skip all the lists of names, and go on to read about the reign of Solomon in 2 Chronicles, but to do so would be a great mistake. Think of the encouragement and guidance these chapters must have given to the Jewish remnant that returned to Jerusalem after the Babylonian captivity. (See the books of Ezra, Nehemiah, Haggai, and Zechariah.) These courageous people had to rebuild the temple and organize its ministry, and reading these chapters would remind them that they were doing

God's work. God gave each detail of the original temple and its ministry to David, who then gave it to Solomon. Those lists of names helped Zerubbabel and Joshua the high priest examine the credentials of those who wanted to serve in the temple (Ezra 2:59–64), and refuse those who were not qualified.

—*Be Restored*, pages 199–200

6. How might 1 Chronicles 22—29 have encouraged the Jews centuries ago? How do individuals matter in the story of God's work in the world? How was that true then? How is it true now?

From the Commentary

Solomon didn't have to draw his own plans for the temple, because the Lord gave the plans to David (1 Chron. 28:11–12). As we read the Word and pray, the Lord shows us His plans for each local church. "Work out your own salvation [Christian ministry] with fear and trembling" (Phil. 2:12–13 NKJV) was written to a congregation of believers in Philippi, and though it has personal application for all believers, the emphasis is primarily on the ministry of the congregation collectively. Some local church leaders run from one seminar to another, seeking to learn how to build the church, when they probably ought to stay home, call the church to prayer, and seek the mind of God in His Word. God has different plans for each church, and we're not supposed to blindly imitate each other.

—*Be Restored*, pages 200–201

7. Why was the temple built? How did it glorify God? Today, God's people are His temple (Eph. 2:19–22). What evidence do we have in our churches that we're glorifying God, if not in the building itself as in Solomon's day?

From the Commentary

David enlisted both Jews and resident aliens (1 Kings 5:13–18) to help construct the temple. This division of David's government was under Adoram (2 Sam. 20:24), also called Adoniram (1 Kings 4:6). The 30,000 Jewish workers cut timber in Lebanon for a month and then returned home for two months, while the 150,000 alien laborers cut and delivered massive stones from the hills, supervised by Jewish foremen (1 Kings 5:13–18; see 9:15–19; 2 Chron. 2:17–18).… We must not think that these resident aliens were treated as slaves, because the law of Moses clearly prohibited such practices (Ex. 22:21; 23:9; Lev. 19:33).

—*Be Restored*, page 202

8. Why was it significant that Gentiles worked alongside the Jews in the building of the temple? How was this a symbol of what was to come in Jesus' day?

More to Consider: Some biblical chronologists believe David was about sixty years old when he inaugurated the temple building program, but we don't know how old Solomon was. David said his son was "young and inexperienced" (1 Chron. 22:5; 29:1), and after his accession to the throne, Solomon called himself "a little child" (1 Kings 3:7). Read 1 Chronicles 22:6–16; 28:9–10, 20–21. How do these verses support the idea that Solomon was young when he began the building project? Why was David anxious to keep the building project moving forward?

From the Commentary

David knew that the ministers of the temple also had to be organized and prepared if God was to be glorified. Too often local church building programs concentrate so much on the financial and the material that they ignore the spiritual, and then a backslidden and divided congregation meets to dedicate the new edifice! A gifted administrator, David organized the Levites (1 Chron. 23), the priests (chap. 24), the temple singers (chap. 25), and the temple officers (chap. 26). David wanted to be sure that everything in God's house would be done "decently and in order" (1 Cor. 14:40 NKJV). In making these decisions, David and his two priests drew lots (1 Chron. 24:5–6, 31; 25:8; 26:13–14, 16). This was the process Joshua used when he gave the tribes their inheritance in the Promised Land (Josh. 14:2; 23:4).

—*Be Restored*, page 204

9. Review 1 Chronicles 23—27. How did David help with the organization and preparation for the temple and its workers? What does the phrase "in the service of the temple of the LORD" mean in these chapters? (See 23:28, 32.) How does that speak to the importance of ministry? What different kinds of ministry do we find in these chapters?

From the Commentary

No amount of human machinery and organization can take the place of heartfelt consecration to the Lord. David was going to leave the scene, an inexperienced son would follow him, and the construction of the temple was a task beyond any one man or group of men. Apart from the blessing of the Lord, the people could not hope to succeed. Leaders come and go, but the Lord remains, and it is the Lord whom we must please.

Like any godly father, David closed his prayer by interceding for his son Solomon, that he would always be obedient to what was written in the law, and that he might succeed in building the temple to the glory of God. ("Palace" in 1 Chronicles 29:19 means "any large palatial structure.") He then called on the congregation to bless the Lord, and they obeyed and bowed low and even fell on their faces in submission and adoration. What a way to begin a building program!

—*Be Restored*, pages 210, 213

10. How did David challenge the leaders in 1 Chronicles 28:1–8? What did he say to Solomon in 28:9–10? How did David convey his gifts for the temple project (28:11—29:9)? How did he call on the Lord (29:11–20)? How did all these activities reveal David's trust in the Lord?

Looking Inward

Take a moment to reflect on all that you've explored thus far in this study of 2 Samuel 23—24 and 1 Chronicles 11:10–41; 21—29. Review your notes and answers and think about how each of these things matters in your life today.

Tips for Small Groups: To get the most out of this section, form pairs or trios and have group members take turns answering these questions. Be honest and as open as you can in this discussion, but most of all, be encouraging and supportive of others. Be sensitive to those who are going through particularly difficult times and don't press for people to speak if they're uncomfortable doing so.

11. What are some of the ways God has trained you for His kingdom work? What does being "trained by God" mean to you? Is the training always easy? Or clear? Explain.

12. What are some ways you glorify God at church? At home? In the workplace? What does it mean to you to glorify God? Does the building you worship in play an important or an unimportant role in that process? Explain.

13. Do you have any "building projects" coming up in your life? This could be a career change, a family-status change, or any other big event. How are you preparing for these events? What role does God play in your preparation? What can you learn from David's preparation for the temple that applies to your situation?

Going Forward

14. Think of one or two things that you have learned that you'd like to work on in the coming week. Remember that this is all about quality, not quantity. It's better to work on one specific area of life and do it well than to work on many and do poorly (or to be so overwhelmed that you simply don't try).

Do you want to glorify God in some way? Be specific. Go back through 2 Samuel 23—24 and 1 Chronicles 11:10–41; 21—29 and put a star next to the phrase or verse that is most encouraging to you. Consider memorizing this verse.

> *Real-Life Application Ideas: David's legacy is ultimately one of a man who was after God's heart. As you head into the next week, take some time to think about what you're doing to pursue God's heart. How do your actions and choices move you toward (or away from) God? Think about the way you live out your faith at work, at home, among strangers, etc. Are there sins holding you back from God? If so, repent from those sins and pursue restoration with God so you can glorify Him in even the smallest pieces of your life.*

Seeking Help

15. Write a prayer below (or simply pray one in silence), inviting God to work on your mind and heart in those areas you've noted in the Going Forward section. Be honest about your desires and fears.

Notes for Small Groups:

- *Look for ways to put into practice the things you wrote in the Going Forward section. Talk with other group members about your ideas and commit to being accountable to one another.*

- *During the coming week, ask the Holy Spirit to continue to reveal truth to you from what you've read and studied.*

Summary and Review

Notes for Small Groups: This session is a summary and review of this book. Because of that, it is shorter than the previous lessons. If you are using this in a small-group setting, consider combining this lesson with a time of fellowship or a shared meal.

Before you begin ...
- *Pray for the Holy Spirit to reveal truth and wisdom as you go through this lesson.*
- *Briefly review the notes you made in the previous sessions. You will refer back to previous sections throughout this bonus lesson.*

Looking Back

1. Over the past eight lessons, you've examined 2 Samuel and 1 Chronicles. What expectations did you bring to this study? In what ways were those expectations met?

2. What is the most significant personal discovery you've made from this study?

3. What surprised you most about 2 Samuel and 1 Chronicles? What, if anything, troubled you?

Progress Report

4. Take a few moments to review the Going Forward sections of the previous lessons. How would you rate your progress for each of the things you chose to work on? What adjustments, if any, do you need to make to continue on the path toward spiritual maturity?

5. In what ways have you grown closer to Christ during this study? Take a moment to celebrate those things. Then think of areas where you feel you still need to grow and note those here. Make plans to revisit this study in a few weeks to review your growing faith.

Things to Pray About

6. The books of 2 Samuel and 1 Chronicles are primarily about David's life and legacy. As you reflect on his victories, defeats, and challenges, consider how you can learn from his experiences to improve your own relationship with God.

7. The messages in 2 Samuel and 1 Chronicles include kindness, discipline, disobedience, hope, and restoration. Spend time praying for each of these topics.

8. Whether you've been studying this in a small group or on your own, there are many other Christians working through the very same issues you discovered when examining 2 Samuel and 1 Chronicles. Take time to pray for them, that God would reveal truth, that the Holy Spirit would guide you, and that each person might grow in spiritual maturity according to God's will.

A Blessing of Encouragement

Studying the Bible is one of the best ways to learn how to be more like Christ. Thanks for taking this step. In closing, let this blessing precede you and follow you into the next week while you continue to marinate in God's Word:

May God light your path to greater understanding as you review the truths found in 2 Samuel and 1 Chronicles and consider how they can help you grow closer to Christ.